Jasper Hopkins, professor of philosophy at the University of Minnesota, is the author of *A Companion to the Study of Saint Anselm*.

Herbert Richardson, professor of theology at Saint Michael's College, University of Toronto, is the author of *Toward an American Theology*.

ANSELM
OF CANTERBURY

VOLUME ONE

Monologion, Proslogion, Debate with Gaunilo,
and a Meditation on Human Redemption

Edited and translated by
Jasper Hopkins and Herbert Richardson

THE EDWIN MELLEN PRESS
Toronto and New York

Library of Congress Catalog Card Number 74-19840
ISBN 0–88946–000–0

First American Edition by The Edwin Mellen Press 1974
Second American Edition by The Edwin Mellen Press 1975
© 1974 SCM Press Ltd, London and The Edwin Mellen Press
Toronto & New York
Printed in Great Britain

CONTENTS

TRANSLATORS' PREFACE

Within the field of medieval philosophy and theology Anselm of Canterbury (1033–1109) has come to be known primarily for his extended arguments in the *Monologion*, *Proslogion*, and *Cur Deus Homo*. In the *Monologion* he ambitiously undertakes to prove – by rational reflection alone, without recourse to the authority of Scripture – that God exists and is consistently triune. He draws upon the insights available in Augustine's *On the Trinity*, adhering to Augustine's distinction between substantial and relational predicates and fastening upon the identification of God with the Good, which all men seek, whether wittingly or unwittingly. The *Monologion* also reiterates Augustine's doctrine of exemplarism by teaching that in the mind of God there is a form (or likeness) of creation, which is logically and causally prior to creation. Finally, Anselm's brief remarks regarding perception, as well as his distinction between words and concepts, are clearly Augustinian.[1] The *Monologion* was Anselm's first systematic treatise, written when he was already forty-three years old. In this treatise he intended to set forth plainly and coherently the rationale for the medieval conception of God as "living, wise, powerful and all-powerful, true, just, blessed, eternal, and whatever similarly is in every respect better than its contradictory."[2]

By comparison, the *Proslogion* is an abridgement of the *Monologion* and represents Anselm's effort to formulate a single line of reasoning (*unum argumentum*) which will demonstrate "that You exist, as we believe, and that You are what we believe You to be."[3] Here Anselm marshals the famous ontological argument, which through the centuries has vexed or dazzled the greatest of minds. Gaunilo's ensuing defense of the Fool afforded Anselm the renewed opportunity to set in array the inexorable logic of his proof. Although in last analysis the proof is unsound, the reasons for its unsoundness are difficult to formulate accurately. Thus, it is not surprising that Gaunilo failed to unmask the argument's flaws – failed, for that matter, even to do justice to the inherent plausibility of the reasoning. For he did not recognize the *reductio ad impossibile* structure of the argument.

If the *Proslogion* constitutes the zenith of Anselm's philosophizing, the *Cur Deus Homo* represents the summit of his theologizing. The theological stance there taken is summarized effectively in *A Meditation on Human Redemption*. In this speculative devotional Anselm makes clear his disaffection with the devil-ransom theory[4] of the atonement, mediated through Augustine's *On the Trinity* 13 and *Free Choice* 3. In its place he develops the theory of satisfaction. According to this theory the Son of God assumed a human nature into His own person, thereby revealing Himself in Jesus and letting Himself be put to death. Because the God-man was sinless, His death was not required; and because it was not required, His voluntary undergoing of death was meritorious. Hence, this merit could be counted by the Father as payment, or satisfaction, for the debt of all men's sins.

Thus, the present volume draws together three of Anselm's works which illustrate his distinctive contributions to eleventh-century philosophy and theology. These three works, perhaps more than any others, serve to introduce the reader to the very spirit of Anselm's thought. For in them Anselm blends, but does not confuse, the conceptual and the devotional. Indeed, the *Monologion*, and its *sola ratione* methodology, was originally entitled *An Example of Meditating about the Rational Basis of Faith*. And the *Proslogion*, first called *Faith Seeking Understanding*, surrounds the ontological argument with prayers and intonings, lamentation and rejoicing, similar to Augustine's elevated style in the *Confessions*. On the other hand, *A Meditation on Human Redemption*, although fundamentally an expression of religious fervor, deliberately includes theological reflection upon the purpose of the incarnation. Thus, Anselm unites the spiritual and the rational in a synthesis which does violence to neither. And this synthesis attests to his conviction – so characteristic of the medieval world – that the spiritual requires the guidance of the rational just as the rational needs the vitality of the spiritual.

Translators' Preface

We are grateful to Friedrich Frommann Press (Stuttgart, Germany) for permission to translate from the critical edition of Anselm's Latin texts edited by F. S. Schmitt.[5] In preparing these translations we have aimed at furnishing a clear statement of what Anselm means, while not veering farther than necessary from his Latin constructions. Thus, although we have not followed Anselm clumsily – word for word, pleonasm for pleonasm, passive sentence for passive sentence – the fact remains that we have been faithful to his actual expressions insofar as readability and intelligibility have allowed.

Jasper Hopkins
Department of Philosophy, University of Minnesota

Herbert Richardson
St Michael's College, University of Toronto

PREVIOUS ENGLISH TRANSLATIONS

M   Monologion
P   Proslogion
OBF   On Behalf of the Fool

R   Reply to Gaunilo
MHR   Meditation on Human Redemption

Anselm of Canterbury, *St Anselm's Book of Meditations and Prayers*, trans. anonymously by M. R., intro. by H. Edward, London: Burns & Oates 1872. (MHR)

— *Prayers and Meditations*, trans. anonymously by a Religious of CSMV, London: A. R. Mowbray & Co. 1952. (MHR)

Charlesworth, M. J., *St Anselm's Proslogion*, Oxford: Oxford University Press 1965. (P; OBF; R)

Deane, S. N., trans. *St Anselm: Basic Writings*, La Salle, Ill.: Open Court, 1962. (1st ed., *St Anselm, Proslogium; Monologium; an Appendix in Behalf of the Fool by Gaunilon; and Cur Deus Homo*, Chicago: Open Court 1903). (Also contains R)

Fairweather, E. R., ed. and trans., *A Scholastic Miscellany: Anselm to Occam*, Philadelphia: Westminster Press and London, SCM Press 1956. (P; excerpt from R)

Hick, J. H., and A. C. McGill, eds., *The Many-faced Argument: Recent Studies of the Ontological Argument for the Existence of God*, London and New York: Macmillan 1967. (excerpt from P; OBF; R)

Maginnis, J. S., "Translations from Anselm," *Bibliotheca Sacra* 8 (July 1851), 529–53. (P)

— "Proofs of the Existence of God. A Reply to Anselm and Anselm's Rejoinder," *Bibliotheca Sacra* 8 (October 1851), 669–715. (OBF; R)

Pegis, A. C., ed. and trans., *The Wisdom of Catholicism*, New York: Random House 1949. (P)

Stanhope, G., *Pious Breathings. Being the Meditations of St Augustine, His Treatise of the Love of God, Soliloquies and Manual. To which Are Added, Select Contemplations from St Anselm and St Bernard*, London 1708, 3rd edition. (MHR, 289–303)

Webb, C. C. J., ed. and trans., *The Devotions of Saint Anselm*, London: Methuen & Co. 1903. (P; MHR, 105–19)

Wippel, J. F., and A. B. Wolter, eds., *Medieval Philosophy: From St Augustine to Nicholas of Cusa*, New York: Free Press 1969. (excerpt from P; OBF; R)

NOTE: Where, for clarification, words from the Latin text have been inserted into the translations, the following rule has been employed: When the Latin term is noted exactly as it appears in the Latin text, parentheses are used; when the case-endings of nouns have been transformed to the nominative, brackets are used.

The numbering of the Psalms accords with the Douay Version and, in parentheses, with the King James (Authorized) Version.

The symbol ∼ indicates negation.

CORRIGENDA

p. 5, line 7:
 Change 'to be in some respect good' to 'in some respect to fare well'.
p. 8, line 23:
 Change 'is' to 'exists'.
p. 9, lines 20-24:
 Change to read: 'Now, if it is nothing other than their essence, then just as their essences are one rather than many, so too the natures are one rather than many. For here I am taking the nature to be identical with the essence.'
p. 11, lines 17-19:
 Literally: 'what is said to exist through something is seen to exist either through something efficient or through matter or through some other aid, as through an instrument.'
p. 66, line 6:
 Change 'without qualification' to 'at all'.
p. 72, line 9 from bottom:
 Change 'Word alone' to 'sole Word'.
p. 82, last line:
 Change 'striving unto' to 'striving for'.
p. 92, last line:
 Change 'begun hungering' to 'in hunger begun'.
Any additional corrections in this series will be listed in Volume IV.

MONOLOGION

Preface

Certain brothers have persisted in urging me to write out for them, in the form of a meditation, a number of things which I had discussed in non-technical terms with them regarding meditating on the Divine Being and regarding various other themes related to a meditation of this kind. For the writing of this meditation they prescribed – in accordance more with their own wishes than with the ease of the task or with my ability – the following format: that nothing at all in the meditation would be argued on Scriptural authority, but that in unembellished style and by uncomplicated arguments and with simplified discussion rational necessity would tersely prove, and truth's clarity would openly manifest, whatever the conclusion of the distinct inquiries declared. They also desired that I not disdain to refute simple and almost foolish objections which would occur to me.

For a long time I was reluctant to attempt any of this; and comparing myself with what was required, I tried on many grounds to make excuses for myself. For the more readily they wished that what they were seeking should be of practical use to them, the more difficult they were making it for me to accomplish what they sought. But at last, overcome by the modest insistence of their entreaties as well as by the commendable probity of their zeal, I began to undertake what they were requesting, even though I was still reluctant because of the difficulty of the assignment and the weakness of my intellectual power. But because of their love I gladly and to the best of my ability finished it in accordance with their prescription. I was induced to this undertaking by the expectation that whatever I did would be known only to those who made the request of me and that after a while they would overwhelm it with contempt, scorning it as a thing of little value. For in this undertaking, I know, I was not so much able to satisfy those who made the request of me as I was able to put an end to the entreaties that

3

pursued me. Nevertheless, contrary to my expectations, it somehow turned out that not only the brothers whom I mentioned but also several others were engaged in committing this treatise to posterity by each making a copy for himself.

After frequent reexamination I have not been able to find that I said in this treatise anything inconsistent with the writings of the Catholic fathers – especially with blessed Augustine's writings. Therefore, if it shall seem to anyone that in this short work I have set forth some doctrine which either is altogether new or else departs from the truth, then I make the following request: Let him not immediately declare me to be one who presumes to new doctrines or who teaches falsehood, but let him first look carefully at the books of *On the Trinity* by the aforementioned teacher, viz., Augustine, and then let him judge my short work by comparison with these books. For in stating that the Supreme Trinity can be called three substances, I have followed the Greeks, who confess that [God is] three substances in one person, by means of the same faith with which we confess that [He] is three persons in one substance.[1] For with respect to God they mean by "substance" what we mean by "person."

Now, whatever I have stated in this treatise I have stated in the role of one who by reflection alone (*sola cogitatione*) investigates, and disputes with himself about, points which he had previously not considered – just as I knew was desired by those whose request I was endeavoring to oblige.

Now, I beseech and adjure anyone who wants to copy this short work to make sure to append this preface at the very front before the chapter-titles themselves. For if someone knows at the outset with what intent and in what manner the discussion has been conducted, I believe that he will be greatly aided in understanding what he will read in the work itself. I also think that if someone sees this preface first, he will not be quick to pass judgment should he find presented [in the treatise] something counter to his own view.

Chapter One: There is something that is the best, the greatest, the highest of all existing things.

There may be someone who, as a result of not hearing or not believing, is ignorant of the one Nature, highest of all existing things, alone sufficient unto itself in its eternal beatitude, through its own omnipotent goodness giving and causing all other things to be something and to be in some respect good. And he may also be ignorant of the many other things which we necessarily believe about God and His creatures. If so, then I think that in great part he can persuade himself of these matters merely by reason alone (*sola ratione*) – if he is of even average intelligence. Although he can do this in many ways, I shall propose one way which I regard as the most accessible for him. For since all men seek to enjoy only those things which they consider good, at some time or other he can readily turn his mind's eye to investigating that thing from whence are derived these goods which he seeks only because he judges them to be good. Thus, with reason guiding and with him following,[2] he may then rationally advance to the matters of which he is unreasonably ignorant. Nevertheless, if in this investigation I say something that a greater authority does not mention, then even if my statement is a necessary consequence of reasons which will seem [good] to me, I want the statement to be accepted as follows: It is not thereby said to be absolutely necessary but is only said to be able to appear necessary for the time being.[3]

It is, then, easy for someone to ask himself the following question: Although the great variety of goods that we perceive through the senses or distinguish through the mind are so numerous, are we to believe that there is one thing through which all good things are good, or are we to believe that different goods are good through different things?[4] Indeed, to all who are willing to give heed, the following is evident and thoroughly certain: Whatever things are called something in such way that they are called it either in greater or lesser or equal degree in

5

relation to one another – they are called it with respect to something in them which is identical (rather than with respect to something different in the different things), whether it be regarded as in them either in equal or in unequal degree. E.g., whatever things are called *just* in relation to one another – whether they are called equally just or whether some are called more just and others less just – can only be understood to be just through justice, which is not something different in these different things. Therefore, since it is certain that all good things are either equally or unequally good when compared with one another, it is necessary that all good things are good with respect to something which is understood to be identical in these various goods – although occasionally some goods seem to be called good with respect to different features. For with respect to one feature a horse seems to be called good because it is strong, and with respect to another feature it seems to be called good because it is swift. Although it seems to be called good with respect to strength and good with respect to swiftness, nevertheless strength and swiftness do not seem to be the same thing. Now, if a horse is good because it is strong or swift, how is it that a strong and swift robber is evil? Rather, then, just as a strong and swift robber is evil because he is harmful, so a strong and swift horse is good because it is useful.[5] Indeed, ordinarily nothing is considered good except because of a certain usefulness (e.g., health and whatever conduces to health are called good) or because of some kind of excellence (e.g., beauty and whatever conduces to beauty are considered good). But since the reasoning already seen can in no way be faulted, it is necessary that every useful and every excellent thing – if they are truly goods – be good through that very thing (whatever it be) through which all goods must be good.

But who could doubt that that through which all goods are good is itself a great good? Therefore, it is good through itself since every good is good through it.[6] So it follows that all other goods are good through something other than what they are and that this other alone is good through itself. But no good which is good through another is equal to or greater than that good which is good through itself. Hence, only that good which alone is good through itself is supremely good; for that is supreme which so excels others that it has neither an equal nor a superior. Now, what is supremely good is also supremely great. Therefore, there is one thing which is supremely good and supremely great – i.e., which is the highest of all existing things.

Chapter Two: The same topic continued.

Just as something has been found to be supremely good inasmuch as all goods are good through some one thing which is good through itself, so it follows necessarily that something is supremely great inasmuch as whatever things are great are great through some one thing which is great through itself. I do not mean great in size, as is a material object; but I mean great[7] in the sense that the greater anything is the better or more excellent it is – as in the case of wisdom. Now, since only what is supremely good can be supremely great, it is necessary that something be both supremely great and supremely good, i.e., the highest of all existing things.

Chapter Three: There is a Nature which exists through itself, which is the highest of all existing things, and through which exists whatever is.

In fact, not only are all goods good through the same thing and all magnitudes great through the same thing but also whatever *is* is seen to exist through some one thing. For whatever is exists either through something or through nothing. But it is not the case that anything exists through nothing. For it cannot even be conceived that there is anything which exists other than through something. Thus, whatever is exists only through something. Accordingly, either there is one thing or there are many things through which all existing things exist. But if there are many things, then either (1) these many derive their existence from some one thing or (2) they exist independently, each through itself, or (3) they exist mutually through themselves ($\sim$1) But if these many existed through one thing, then it would not be the case that everything exists through a plurality, but would rather be the case that everything exists through that one thing through which the many exist. ($\sim$2) But if the many existed independently, each through itself, then surely there would be some one power (*vis*) or nature (*natura*) of existing *per se* which they would have in order to exist through themselves. And there is no doubt that they would exist through that one power or nature to which they would owe the fact of their existing through themselves.[8] Thus, whatever is would exist through this one thing more truly than through the many things which themselves could not exist without this one. (∼3) But [sound] reasoning does not allow that the many exist mutually through themselves, for the thought that one thing exists through another to which it gives existence is irrational. For not even relational things exist in this manner through one another. For example, when a master and a servant are referred to relatively to each other, the two men referred to do not at all exist through each other, nor do the relations by which they are referred to exist at all through each other (for these relations exist through their subjects).

Therefore, since the truth altogether excludes the possibility that there is a plurality through which all things exist, there must be one thing through which all existing things exist.

Since, then, all existing things exist through one thing, without doubt this one thing exists through itself. Thus, all things other than this one exist through another, and this one alone exists through itself. But whatever exists through another is less than that which alone exists through itself and through which all other things exist. Accordingly, that which exists through itself exists most greatly of all. Therefore, there is some one thing which alone exists most greatly and most highly of all. But what exists most greatly of all and is that through which exists whatever is good and great and whatever is anything at all – this must be supremely good, supremely great, the highest of all existing things. For this reason, there is something which – whether it is called a being, a substance, or a nature[9] – is the best and the greatest and the highest of all existing things.

Chapter Four: The same topic continued.

Moreover, if anyone considers the natures of things, he cannot help perceiving that they are not all of equal worth but that some are distinguished by a greater or lesser degree of worth than others.[10] For if anyone doubts that a horse is by nature better than a piece of wood and that a man is more excellent than a horse, then surely such a person ought not to be called a man. So although we cannot deny that some natures are better than others, nonetheless reason persuades us that one of them is so preeminent that no other nature is superior to it. For if such an order of gradation were so limitless that for each degree a higher degree could be found, then reason would be led to the conclusion that the number of these natures is infinite. But everyone holds such a view to be absurd, except someone who himself is utterly foolish. Therefore, necessarily, there is a nature which is so superior to any other or others that there is no nature to which it is ranked as inferior.

But this nature which is thus supreme is singular – or else there is more than one nature of this kind, all of which are equal. Assume that they are many and equal. Since they cannot be equal through different things but only through the same thing, this one thing through which they are equally so great either is itself what they are (i.e., it is their essence) or else is something other than what they are. Now, if it were identical with their essence, then just as their essence would be singular rather than plural, so their nature would be singular rather than plural. For in the present context I understand a nature to be the same thing as an essence. On the other hand, if that through which these many natures are equally great were other than what they are, surely they would be less than that through which they are great. For whatever is great through another is less than that other through which it is great. Therefore, they would not be so great that nothing else is greater than they. Now, if neither through what they are nor through another it is possible for there to be many equal natures than which nothing else is more excellent, then there cannot at all be a plurality of such natures. Therefore, it follows, there is only one Nature which is so superior to all others that it is inferior to none. Now, a thing of this kind is the greatest and the best of all existing things. Thus, there is a Nature which is the highest of all existing things.

But it can be the highest only if through itself it is what it is and only if through *it* all other existing things are what they are. For a few moments ago reason taught that that which exists through itself and through which all other things exist is the highest of all existing things. Consequently, either that which is the highest of all exists through itself and all other things exist through it (the converse of the preceding statement),[11] or else there are many supreme beings. But it has been established that there cannot be many supreme beings. Hence, there is a Nature, or Substance, or Being (*essentia*)[12] which through itself is good and great, and through itself is what it is; and through this Nature exists whatever truly is good or great or something. And this Nature is the Supreme Good, the Supreme Greatness, the Supreme Being (*ens*), or Subsistence (*subsistens*) – in short, the highest of all existing things.

Chapter Five: Just as this Nature exists through itself (*per se*) and all else exists through it, so it exists from itself (*ex se*) and all else exists from it.

Since, then, our discoveries so far have been rewarding, it is agreeable to investigate (1) whether or not this Nature exists from, as well as through, itself and (2) whether or not whatever is something exists from, as well as through, this Nature. Clearly, what exists from something can likewise be said to exist through it; and what exists through something can likewise be said to exist from it. For example, what is from matter and through a craftsman can also be said to be through matter and from a craftsman. For through both and from both (i.e., by both) it has its existence, even though the way it exists through matter and from matter is not the same as the way it exists through a craftsman and from a craftsman. As a logical consequence, then: Just as whatever is is what it is through the Supreme Nature, and thus this Nature exists through itself, whereas all else exists through another – so whatever is is from the Supreme Nature, and thus this Nature exists from itself, whereas all else exists from another.

Chapter Six: This Nature was not brought into existence
through the assistance of any cause. Nevertheless, it does not exist through nothing or from
nothing. How it can be understood to be
through itself and from itself.

Therefore, since neither "to be through something" nor "to be
from something" always has the same sense, we must inquire
more carefully how whatever is exists through and from the
Supreme Nature. And since what exists through itself does not
have the same mode of existing as what exists through another,
let us separately examine first the Supreme Nature, which exists
through itself, and afterwards those things which exist through
another.

Therefore, since it is evident that this Nature is through itself
whatever it is and that through it all other things are what they
are, in what manner does this Nature exist through itself? For
what is said to exist through something seems to exist through it
either efficiently or materially or *instrumentally* (i.e., in such way
that the other is a kind of *aid*).[13] But whatever exists in any of
these three modes exists through another and is later and somehow less than this other through which it has its existence. Yet,
the Supreme Nature does not at all exist through another; nor
is it later or less than itself or any other. For this reason, the
Supreme Nature could not have been [efficiently] caused to
exist by itself or by another; nor was it itself or anything else
the material from which it was made; nor did it somehow aid
itself or receive aid from anything else so that [by either aid]
it should become what it previously was not.

What [shall we say] then? For what did not come to exist by
anything's having [efficiently] caused it or from any matter or
by means of any assisting [i.e., instrumental] causes seems either
to be nothing or, if it is something, to exist through nothing
(*per nihil*) and from nothing (*ex nihilo*). Although (on the basis
of what I have already noticed about the Supreme Substance by
the light of reason) I think that these implications do not at all
apply to this Substance, nonetheless I will not neglect con-
structing a proof of this point. For since this meditation of mine

has led me all of a sudden to a certain important and interesting point, I do not want to pass over carelessly even some simple, almost foolish, objection occurring to me in my discussion. For if I leave nothing doubtful in the preceding arguments, I can advance more assuredly to the succeeding ones; and if I hope to convince someone of what I observe, then by my removing every obstacle, including small ones, even a person slow to understand can have easy access to what he has heard.

Therefore, to say that this Nature (without which no nature could exist) is nothing is as false as it would be absurd to say that whatever exists is nothing. Moreover, this Nature does not exist *through* nothing, since it is inconceivable that what is something should exist through nothing. Yet, if this Nature somehow existed *from* nothing, then it would have to exist from nothing either (1) through itself or (2) through another or (3) through nothing.

(~3) Now, it has been established that something does not at all exist *through* nothing. So if this Nature somehow existed *from* nothing, it would have to exist from nothing either through itself or through some other. (~1) But a thing cannot through itself exist from nothing; for if a thing existed from nothing through something, then that through which it existed would have to be prior to it. Therefore, since this Being is not prior to itself, it is not the case that *through itself* it somehow exists from nothing.

(~2) On the other hand, if this Nature be said to have come from nothing through some other nature, then this Nature would not be the highest of all but would be inferior to some other; moreover it would not through itself be what it is, but would be it through another. Likewise, if this Nature existed from nothing through something else, then this something through which it existed would have been a great good since it would have been the cause of such great good. But no good could conceivably have existed before the Good without which nothing at all would be good. Now, it is clear enough that this Good, without which nothing at all would be good, is identical with the Supreme Nature which is under discussion. Hence, it is not even conceivable that this Nature could have been preceded by some other thing through which it existed from nothing.[14]

Finally, if this Nature were something either *through* nothing or *from* nothing, then without doubt either it would not be through and from itself whatever it is or else it would [have to] be said to be nothing. But it is superfluous to discuss how false each of these alternatives is. Therefore, even though the Supreme Substance does not exist through anything efficiently or from anything materially, and was not helped to begin existing by any [instrumental] causes, nevertheless it does not at all exist through nothing or from nothing, because whatever it is it is through and from itself.

How, then, in the last analysis, ought this Nature to be understood to exist through itself and from itself if it did not [efficiently] cause itself and did not come from its own matter and did not somehow aid itself to become what earlier it was not? Should we perhaps understand how, by comparison with our saying that through itself and from itself light shines and is something shining? For in the way that *light* and *to shine* and *shining* are related to one another, so *what is* (*essentia*) and *to be* and *being* (i.e., *existing*, or *subsisting*)[15] are related to one another. Thus, *supreme being* and *supremely to be* and *supremely being* (i.e., *supremely existing*, or *subsisting*) are analogous to *light* and *to shine* and *shining*.[16]

Chapter Seven: How all other things are through and from this Nature.

Now, with regard to all the things which exist through another, there remains to discuss how they exist through the Supreme Substance: do they exist through it (A) because it [efficiently] caused them or (B) because it was the matter of all these things? We need not ask whether or not all these things exist through this Substance only by virtue of its having in some way aided them to exist, while something other than this Substance created them or was the material out of which they were made. [We need not pursue such an inquiry] because if all other things existed only secondarily and not principally through this Substance, then what has already been proved would be contradicted.

So I think that I must first ask (B) whether everything which exists through another exists from some matter. I do not doubt that the world's entire mass, as we see it formed with its parts, consists of earth, water, air, and fire. These four elements some-how can be conceived apart from the forms which we see in formed things, so that the unformed, or even mingled, nature of these elements is seen to be the matter of all corporeal objects which exist separately, each having its own form. Although I do not doubt any of these facts, I do ask: Whence comes the aforementioned material of the massive world? For if this material comes from some other matter, then this other is more truly the matter of every corporeal thing. Thus, if all things, whether visible or invisible, come from some matter, then surely they could only be, and be said to be, from the matter (B.1) of the Supreme Nature or (B.2) of themselves, or (B.3) of some third being. (∼B.3) But surely such a third something does not exist. For nothing at all can even be thought to exist except the Supreme Being, which exists through itself, and all other things, which exist through the Supreme Being rather than through themselves. Consequently, what in no way is something is not the matter of anything. (∼B.2) Moreover, the universe, which does not exist through itself, cannot exist from out of its own nature. For if it existed from out of its own nature, it *would* in some way exist through itself and [thus] through something other than that through which all things exist, and that through which all things exist would not be singular. But these alter-natives are false. Moreover, everything that is from matter is from another and is later than that other. Therefore, since nothing is different from itself or later than itself, it follows that nothing exists materially from itself.

(∼B.1) But if from the matter of the Supreme Nature there could be something less than the Supreme Nature, then the Supreme Good could be changed and corrupted – something abominable to say. Thus, since everything other than the Supreme Nature is less than it is, something other than it cannot exist materially from it. Furthermore, assuredly, that through which the Supreme Good would be changed or corrupted would itself not at all be good. But if any nature inferior [to the Supreme Nature] existed from the matter of the Supreme Good, then since whatever exists from anywhere at all exists only through the Supreme Being, the Supreme Good would be changed and corrupted through the Supreme Being. Thus, the Supreme Being, which itself is the Supreme Good, would not be a good at all – an inconsistency. Therefore, no nature inferior [to the Supreme Nature] exists materially from the Supreme Nature. Since, then, it has been established that the being of those things which exist through another does not exist materially from the Supreme Being or from itself or from some third thing, it is obvious that (∼B) it does not exist from any matter.

Therefore, since whatever is exists through the Supreme Being, and since all things other than the Supreme Being can exist through it only if it either [efficiently] causes them or else is the matter out of which they are made, necessarily (A) nothing else besides it exists except by its [efficiently] causing. And since there neither is nor was anything except this Being and the things produced by it, this Being was not able to produce anything at all through anything else (be it merely an instrument or an aid) than through itself. Yet, everything that it created it created, without doubt, either (A.1) from something material, or else (A.2) from nothing. Therefore, since it is most assuredly obvious that the being of all existing things (other than the Supreme Being) has been created by the Supreme Being and (∼A.1) exists from no matter, assuredly nothing is more clear than that (A.2) the Supreme Being through itself and by itself produced from nothing (*ex nihilo*) so great a complex of things – so vastly numerous, so beautifully formed, so well-ordered in their variety, so harmonious in their diversity.

Chapter Eight: What is meant by "[This Nature] made all things from nothing."

But a problem occurs about *nothing*.[17] For that from which some thing is made is a cause of the thing made from it; and, necessarily, every cause contributes some assistance to the effect's existence. On the basis of their experience all men accept this [principle] – to such an extent that it can be wrested from no one through debate, and from scarcely no one through deception. Hence, if something were made from nothing, nothing was a cause of what was made from it. Yet, how is it that what had no existence aided something else to begin to exist? But if no aid comes to something from nothing, who can be persuaded, and how can he be persuaded, that something is made from nothing?

Moreover, either "nothing" signifies something or it does not signify something. If nothing is something, then whatever has been made from nothing has been made from something. But if nothing is not something, then from nothing nothing is made; for it is inconceivable that anything be made from nothing at all. (As the truism goes: "From nothing nothing comes.") Therefore, it seems to follow that whatever is made is made from something. For a thing is made either from something or from nothing. Therefore, whether nothing is something or whether it is not something, whatever has been made must (it seems) have been made from something. However, if this conclusion is posited as true, it opposes all the conclusions previously reached. Accordingly, since what was nothing would be something, that which was the greatest something would be nothing. For from the fact that I found a certain substance which exists most greatly of all, I rationally inferred that all things other than this Substance were made by it in such way that they were made from nothing. Therefore, if that from which they were made (which I believed to be nothing) is something, then all that I thought I had concluded about the Supreme Being would be nothing.[18]

What, then, must be understood about *nothing*? For I have already determined not to neglect in this meditation any objection which I see to be possible – even an almost foolish objection. So if any substance is said to have been made from nothing, this statement can be interpreted in three ways; and these interpretations suffice to resolve the present difficulty. One way is that by which we want it understood that what is said to have been made from nothing has not at all been made. This is similar to the case in which one asks about another who is silent, "Of what is he speaking?" and is given the reply "Of nothing"; that is, the other is not speaking. In this sense one who asks with regard to the Supreme Being or with regard to something which has not at all existed and does not at all exist, "From what was it made?", can correctly be answered "From nothing." That is, it was not made at all. This sense can be understood of none of the things which have been made. Secondly, there is a signification of "from nothing" which can be expressed but yet which cannot be the case. For example, something may be said to have been made from nothing in that it was made from nothing itself (i.e., from what does not at all exist), as if nothing itself were an existing thing from which some other thing could be made.[19] But since this statement is always false, a contradiction ensues as often as the statement is asserted. The third interpretation by which something is said to have been made from nothing is when we understand that it has in fact been made but that there is not anything from which it was made. The signification is seen to be similar when of a man who is saddened without reason we say, "He is saddened from nothing." Therefore, if we construe in this third sense our previous conclusion that except for the Supreme Being all existing things have been made by the Supreme Being from nothing – i.e., not from anything – then just as that conclusion follows consistently from the preceding argument, so from that conclusion nothing inconsistent follows.

We can say suitably and without any inconsistency that those things which have been made by the Creative Substance were made from nothing – in the way we commonly say that a rich man has been made from a poor man, or that from sickness a man has regained health. That is, he who previously was poor is now rich – something which he was not beforehand; and he who previously was sick is now healthy – something which he was not beforehand. In this [same] manner, then, we can fittingly understand the following statements: "The Creative Being has made all things from nothing" and "Through the Creative Being all things have been made from nothing" – that is, things that once were nothing are now something. And in saying that the Creative Being *made* or that all other things *were made*, we mean that when the Creative Being made, it made something, and that when the other things were made, they were made only something. Thus, when we observe a man of meager means who has been elevated by a second man to great wealth or honor, we say "The second man has made the first man from nothing," or "The first man was made from nothing by the second man." That is, the first man, who formerly was regarded as nothing, is now esteemed as truly something because of the making of the second man.

Chapter Nine: Before their creation those things which have
been made from nothing were not nothing with
respect to the thought (*rationem*) of their Maker.

But I seem to see a certain point which compels me to distinguish carefully the respect in which those things which have
been made can be said to have been nothing before they were
made. For by no means can anything reasonably be made by
anyone unless beforehand there is in the thought (*ratione*) of
the maker a certain pattern, as it were, of the thing to be made –
or more suitably put, a form or likeness or rule. Thus, it is
evident that before all things were made there was in the thought
of the Supreme Nature what they were going to be or what kind
they were going to be or how they were going to be.[20] Therefore,
although it is clear that before they were made, those things
which have been made were nothing – with respect to the fact
that they were not then what they are now and that there was
not anything from which they were made – nevertheless they
were not nothing with respect to their Maker's thought, through
which and according to which they were made.

Chapter Ten: This thought (*ratio*) is an expression of things,
just as a craftsman first tells himself what he is
going to make.

But what is this form of things, which in the Maker's thought
preceded the things to be created, other than a conceptual
expression[21] of things? – just as when a craftsman[22] who is
about to make a work from his craft first speaks of it within himself by a mental conception? Now, by "mental expression" or
"conceptual expression" I do not mean here thinking the words
which are significative of things; I mean, rather, viewing mentally with keenness of thought the things themselves which
either already exist or else are going to exist. For in ordinary
usage we recognize that we can speak of a single object in three
ways. For we may speak of it either (1) by perceptibly employing

perceptible signs (i.e., signs which can be perceived by the bodily senses) or (2) by imperceptibly thinking to ourselves these same signs, which are perceptible outside us, or (3) neither by perceptibly nor by imperceptibly using these signs, but by inwardly and mentally speaking of the objects themselves by imagining them or by understanding their respective definitions, depending upon the type of object.[23] For in one way I speak of a man when I signify him by the name "man." In another way [I speak of him] when I think this name silently. In a third way [I speak of a man] when my mind beholds him either by means of an image of his body or by means of his definition – by means of an image of his body, for instance, when [my mind] imagines his visible shape; but by means of his definition, for instance, when [my mind] conceives his universal being, viz., *rational, mortal animal.*[24]

Each of these three kinds of speaking has its corresponding kind of word. Yet, words of that kind of speaking which I mentioned third, and last, are natural and are the same for all races, provided they are not words of unknown things.[25] And since all other words have been formulated because of these natural words, wherever these are no other word need be present for recognizing an object; and where they cannot be, no other word is useful for manifesting the object. Moreover, these natural words can without absurdity be called truer the more they resemble, and the more expressly they signify, the objects for which they are words. Except for those things which we use as names for themselves in order to signify themselves (e.g., certain sounds such as the vowel *a*) – except for these, I say – no other word seems so similar to the object for which it is a word, and no other word so expresses that object, as does that likeness which is expressed in the acuteness of the mind as it conceives the object itself. Therefore, the natural word is rightly and especially to be called the proper and principal word for an object. No expression of anything whatsoever more closely approximates an object than that which is present in natural words; and in no one's thought can there be anything else which is so similar to an object, whether already existing or going to exist. Consequently, in the case of the Supreme Substance such an Expression of objects can justifiably be seen (1) to have existed before these objects, in order that they might be made through it, and (2) to exist now that they have been made, in order that they might be known through it.

Chapter Eleven: Nevertheless, this comparison contains many differences.

It is true that the Supreme Substance spoke within itself, as it were, all creatures before it created them through and according to its own inmost Expression – just as a craftsman first conceives mentally what he subsequently produces in accordance with his mental conception. But even though this is true, I detect in this comparison many differences [between the Supreme Substance and an ordinary craftsman]. For the Supreme Substance did not from anywhere borrow anything at all whereby to fashion in itself the form of the creatures which it was going to make, or whereby to make these creatures what they are. By contrast, an artisan cannot at all conceive in his mind, imaginatively, any material object except one which he has already in some way experienced (either in its entirety all at once or through parts) from various objects.[26] Moreover, an artisan cannot produce the work conceived in his mind if he lacks either the materials or some thing without which the preconceived work cannot be accomplished. For although a man can form the concept or the image of some kind of animal which has never existed, he can do so only by putting together parts which he remembers from his experience of other objects.[27] Hence, these two inner expressions of their respective works to be made – viz., the Expression in the Creative Substance and the expression in an artisan – differ from each other in the following respect: The former was neither borrowed from anywhere nor aided from anywhere; as first and only cause it was able to suffice its Artisan for accomplishing His work. By contrast, the latter is neither the first cause, the sole cause, nor the sufficient cause for commencing his work. Therefore, those things which have been made through the Expression of the Creative Substance are wholly through this Expression whatever they are, whereas things made through an artisan's expression would not at all exist unless they were something more than what they are through his expression.

Chapter Twelve: The Expression of the Supreme Being is
the Supreme Being.

But it is equally certain, as reason teaches, that (1) whatever the
Supreme Substance made, it made only through itself and that
(2) whatever it made, it made through its own inmost Expression
(whether by uttering different things with different words or
rather by uttering all things at once with a single word). Accordingly, what view can be seen to be more necessary than that the
Expression of the Supreme Being is identical with the Supreme
Being? Therefore, I think that examination of this Expression
must not be passed over lightly. But before this topic can be
developed critically, several properties of the Supreme Substance
must be carefully examined, it seems to me.

Chapter Thirteen: As all things were created through the
Supreme Being, so they are sustained
through it.

Therefore, it is evident that whatever is not identical with the
Supreme Nature was made through the Supreme Nature. Only
an irrational mind can doubt that all created things endure and
continue to exist as long as they do because they are sustained by
the same one who created them from nothing and to whom they
owe what they are. We can prove that whatever is sustained [in
existence] is sustained by some one thing which alone is sustained through itself, while everything else is sustained through
another. We can prove this by using an argument similar in
every respect to the argument by which we inferred that whatever is exists through one thing which alone exists through itself,
while everything else exists through another. Since it can only
be the case that [all] the things which have been made are sustained through another and that the thing which has made
them is sustained through itself, it must be the case that just as
nothing was made except through the creative and present
Being, so nothing is sustained except through the conserving
presence of this same Being.

Chapter Fourteen: The Supreme Being is in all things and
through all things; and all things are from
it, through it, and in it.

But if [the above consideration] is true – or rather, because it
must be true – it follows that where the Supreme Being does not
exist, nothing exists. Therefore, the Supreme Being exists everywhere and is through everything and in everything. Now, it is
absurd [to think] that just as a created thing cannot at all exceed
the greatness of the Creating and Sustaining Being, so the
Creating and Sustaining Being cannot at all exceed the totality
of created things. Consequently, it is clear that this Being is
what sustains, excels, limits, and pervades all other things.
Therefore, if these conclusions are conjoined with the ones we
discovered earlier, then one and the same Being exists in and
through all other things and is that from which, through which,
and in which all other things exist.[28]

Chapter Fifteen: What can and cannot be predicated of the
Supreme Being substantively.

Now, I am especially and not unjustifiably moved to inquire, as
earnestly as I can, into what (from among whatever is predicable
of something) can appropriately be predicated substantively of
such a marvellous Nature as this. For I would be surprised if
among the names or words which we apply to things created
from nothing, there could be found a term appropriately predicable of the Substance which created all other things. Nevertheless, we must try to ascertain the conclusion to which reason
will direct this investigation. Now, about relational terms – no
one doubts that none of them applies to the substance of the
thing of which they are predicated relationally.[29] Therefore, if
some term is predicated of the Supreme Nature relationally,
this term does not signify its substance. Thus, although the
Supreme Nature can be spoken of relationally as *supreme* over
all things or as *greater* than all things which it created (or spoken
of relationally in some other similar way), [these utterances] do

not, it is obvious, designate its natural being.[30] For if there never had existed any of the things in relation to which it is called greater and supreme, then it could not be understood to be greater or supreme. Nevertheless, it would not for that reason be less good or would not undergo any detriment at all with respect to its essential greatness. We recognize this plainly from the fact that through no other than through itself is this Being as good as it is or as great as it is. So if the Supreme Nature can so be understood to be not-supreme that it is still understood to be no greater or lesser than when it is understood to be supreme over all things, clearly "supreme" does not signify unqualifiedly, or absolutely (*simpliciter*), that Being which in every way is greater and better than whatever is not what it is. Now, what reason teaches regarding the word "supreme" holds equally true for similar relational terms.

And so, leaving aside those terms which are predicated relatively (since none of them unqualifiedly exhibits the essence of anything), let us turn our attention to the discussion of other terms. Surely, if someone carefully examines one at a time whatever non-relational characteristics there are, each one either is such that it is in every respect (*omnino*) better than its contradictory or else is such that its contradictory is in some respect better than it. (By a characteristic and its contradictory I have in mind here only characteristics such as true and not-true, corporeal and not-corporeal, and the like). Indeed, [in some cases] a characteristic is in every respect better than its contradictory – as, for example, wise than not-wise; i.e., wise is better than not-wise. (For although to be just without being wise seems better than to be wise without being just, nevertheless "Not-wise is better than wise" is not unqualifiedly true. But, in fact, "Anything not-wise, with respect to the fact that it is not-wise, is less than anything wise" is unqualifiedly true; for anything not-wise would be better if it were wise.) Likewise, the characteristic true is in every respect better than not-itself, i.e., than not-true; and the characteristic just [is in every respect better] than not-just; and living [is in every respect better] than not-living. But [in some cases] the contradictory of a characteristic is in some respect better than that characteristic; for example, not-gold [is in some respect better] than gold. For it is better for a man to be not-gold than to be gold, even though for something else it would be better to be gold than not-gold (e.g., for lead). For although neither a man nor a piece of lead is gold, still, the more inferior a man's nature would become if the man were gold, the better thing a man is than gold; and the more valuable a piece of lead would become if it were gold, the more inferior lead is to gold.

From the fact that the Supreme Nature can be understood to be not-supreme in such way that (1) for it to be supreme is in no respect better than for it to be not-supreme and (2) for it to be not-supreme is not in some respect better than for it to be supreme, clearly there are many relational terms which are not encompassed by the above classification. I forego inquiring about whether some relational terms *are* so encompassed, because for my purposes what has already been learned about relational terms suffices, viz., that none of these terms designates the simple substance of the Supreme Nature. So if we look separately at whatever terms are not relational, [each indicates a property which] either it is better to be than not to be or else in some respect it is better not to be than to be. Consequently, just as it is blasphemous to suppose that the substance of the Supreme Nature is something which in some respect it would be better not to be, so this substance must be whatever in every respect it is better to be than not to be.[31] For this substance alone is that than which nothing at all is better; and it alone is better than all things which are not what it is. Hence, it is not a material object or one of the things which the bodily senses detect. Indeed, there is something which is not what material objects are and yet which is better than they are. For [consider] a rational mind, whose nature, quality, or quantity is perceived by no bodily sense: The more inferior a rational mind would become if it were one of those things which are subject to the bodily senses, the greater it is than any of those things. For the Supreme Being must in no respect be said to be one of those things to which something that is not what they are is superior. And the Supreme Being (as reason teaches) must unqualifiedly be said to be any of those things to which whatever is not what they are is inferior.[32] Therefore, necessarily, the Supreme Being is living, wise, powerful and all-powerful, true, just, blessed, eternal, and whatever similarly is in every respect better than its contradictory. Why, then, should we continue to ask what this Supreme Nature is, if whatever it is or is not is evident?

Chapter Sixteen: For the Supreme Being to be just is the
same as for it to be justice. The same type
of identity holds for other predicates of a
similar kind. None of these predicates
indicates the quality or the quantity of this
Being, but they indicate what it is.

But when we call the Supreme Being just or great (or any such
thing), perhaps we are indicating what kind of thing it is or how
great it is rather than indicating what it is [i.e., its essence].
Indeed, predicates such as "just" and "great" seem to be predicated with respect to quality and quantity; for whatever is
just is just through justice (and likewise for other predicates of
this kind). Therefore, the Supreme Nature is just only through
justice. Hence, it seems that the supremely good Substance is
called just by participation in the quality of justice. But if so
[i.e., if the Supreme Substance were just in this way], then the
Supreme Substance would be just through another and not
through itself. But this view is contrary to the truth which we
have already seen, viz., that whether good or great or existing –
what [the Supreme Nature] is, it is completely through itself and
not through another. So if it is just only through justice, and if it
can only be just through itself, what is more clear and more
necessary than that this Nature is itself justice? And when it is
said to be just through justice, is not this the same as [being just]
through itself? And when it is said to be just through itself, what
else is meant except that [it is just] through justice?[33] Therefore,
if someone asks "What is this Supreme Nature which you are
investigating?" is there a truer answer than "It is justice"?
So we must look into how we are to understand the statement
that this Nature (which is itself justice) is just.

For since a man cannot be justice but can have justice, a just
man is understood to be one who has justice rather than one who
is justice. So since the Supreme Nature is not properly said to
have justice but to exist as justice, then when it is called just,
it is properly understood to exist as justice rather than to be
something having justice. Hence, if when we say that it exists as
justice we are saying not what kind of thing it is but rather what
it is, then (by logical inference) when we say that it is just, we

25

are saying not what kind of thing it is but what it is. Finally, with regard to the Supreme Being, since to say that it is just is the same as saying that it exists as justice, and since to say that it exists as justice is the same as saying that it is justice, there is no difference between calling it just and calling it justice. Therefore, when someone asks "What is this Nature?" the answer "It is justice" is as appropriate as the answer "It is just."

The intellect is bound to perceive rationally that what we see to have been established in the case of justice also holds true for all the characteristics predicated similarly of the Supreme Nature. Hence, whichever of these characteristics is predicated of this Nature, they tell neither what kind of thing this Nature is nor how great it is but rather what it is. But obviously the Supreme Nature is supremely whatever good thing it is. Therefore, the Supreme Nature is the Supreme Being (*summa essentia*), Supreme Life (*summa vita*), Supreme Reason, Supreme Security (*salus*), Supreme Justice, Supreme Wisdom, Supreme Truth, Supreme Goodness, Supreme Greatness, Supreme Beauty, Supreme Immortality, Supreme Incorruptibility, Supreme Immutability, Supreme Beatitude, Supreme Eternity, Supreme Power, Supreme Unity. And all these descriptions are the same as the descriptions Supremely Being (*summe ens*), Supremely Living (*summe vivens*), and so forth.

Chapter Seventeen: [The Supreme Being] is so simple that anything which can be said of its essence is one and the same in it. And something can be predicated substantively of the Supreme Being only with respect to what it is.

What, then? If the Supreme Nature is so many goods, will it be composed of so many goods, or are they, rather than being many goods, only one good signified by so many names? For everything composite needs for its existence the parts of which it is composed; and what it is it owes to its parts. For through them it is whatever it is, whereas what they are they are not through it; and so it is not at all supreme. Hence, if the Supreme Nature were composed of many goods, then what holds true of

26

everything composite would also have to hold true of it. But the whole necessity of previously established truth destroys and overthrows, by means of a clear argument, this blasphemous falsity. Therefore, since this Nature is in no respect composite and yet is in every respect those many goods [listed above], all those goods must be one rather than many.[34] Hence, any one of them is the same as all the others – whether they be considered separately or all together. For example, when [this Nature] is called justice or being, these predicates signify the same thing as do the other predicates, taken either separately or all together. Thus, even as whatever is predicated essentially of the Supreme Substance is one, so whatever the Supreme Substance is essentially it is in one way, in one respect. For when a man is said to be a body and rational and a human being, these three things are not said in the same way, in the same respect. In one respect he is a body, in another rational; and neither of these constitutes the whole of what a human being is. By contrast, the Supreme Being is not at all anything in such way that there is some other manner or some other respect in which it is not that thing; for whatever the Supreme Being in some respect essentially is, it is as a whole. Therefore, whatever is predicated truly of its essence applies to what it is, not to what kind it is (*qualis*) or to how great it is (*quanta*).[35] For whatever is [subject to] quality or quantity is something else with respect to what it is [i.e., with respect to its essence], and thus is not simple but composite.

Chapter Eighteen: [The Supreme Being] is without beginning and without end.

From what time, then, did this so simple Nature – Creator and Sustainer of all things – first exist? And when will it cease to exist? Or is this Nature neither from a beginning point nor to an end point but rather beginningless and endless? Were it to have a beginning it would have a beginning either (1) from and through itself, (2) from and through another, or (3) from and through nothing. But from the truth already seen, clearly this Nature does not in any way exist either from another or from nothing, either through another or through nothing. Therefore, it did not at all have a beginning from or through another, from or through nothing. Moreover, it could not have had a beginning from or through itself, even though it exists from itself and through itself. For this Nature exists from and through itself in such way that there is not at all one being which exists from and through itself and another being through which and from which the first being exists. Now, whatever begins to exist from something or through something is not at all the same thing as that from which or through which it begins to exist. Therefore, the Supreme Nature did not begin to exist through itself or from itself. Thus, since it has no beginning either ($\sim$1) through or from itself, either ($\sim$2) through or from another, either ($\sim$3) through or from nothing, it has no beginning at all.

On the other hand, [the Supreme Nature] will also have no end. For if it were going to have an end, it would not be supremely immortal and supremely incorruptible. But we have demonstrated that it is both supremely immortal and supremely incorruptible.[36] Hence, it will not have an end. Furthermore, if it were going to have an end, it would come to an end either willingly or unwillingly. But surely that being by means of whose will the Supreme Good perished could not be absolutely good (*simplex bonum*). But the Supreme Nature *is* a true and absolute (*simplex*) good. Hence, this Nature, which is assuredly the Supreme Good, would not come to an end willingly. Yet, if it were going to come to an end unwillingly, it would not be supremely powerful or all-powerful. But rational necessity has already proven that it is supremely powerful and all-powerful. Hence, it would not come to an end unwillingly. Consequently, if the Supreme Nature shall not come to an end either willingly or unwillingly, it shall not at all have an end.

Moreover, if the Supreme Nature were to have a beginning or an end it would not be true eternity – something which we have already uncontestably found it to be.[37] Or again, let anyone who can, try to conceive of when it began to be true, or was ever not true, that something was going to exist.[38] Or [let him try to conceive of] when it will cease being true and will not be true that something has existed in the past. Now, if neither of these things can be conceived, and if both statements can be true only if there is truth, then it is impossible even to think that truth has a beginning or an end. Indeed, suppose that truth had had a beginning, or suppose that it would at some time come to an end:

Then even before truth had begun to be, it would have been true that there was no truth; and even after truth had come to an end, it would still be true that there would be no truth. But it could not be true without truth. Hence, there would have been truth before truth came to be, and there would still be truth after truth had ceased to be. But these conclusions are self-contradictory. Therefore, whether truth is said to have a beginning or an end, or whether it is understood not to have a beginning or an end, truth cannot be confined by any beginning or end. Consequently, the same conclusion holds with regard to the Supreme Nature, because the Supreme Nature is the Supreme Truth.

Chapter Nineteen: How nothing existed before or will exist after the Supreme Being.

But, behold, *nothing* once again rises up; and it alleges to be nothing all that reason has thus far discussed and all that truth and necessity have given consistent witness to. For if those things which have been explained above have been made secure by the fortification of necessary truth, then there was not anything earlier than the Supreme Being nor will there be anything later than the Supreme Being. Hence, nothing was before it and nothing will be after it. For either something or nothing must have preceded it and must be going to succeed it. But anyone who says that nothing was prior to it and that nothing will be subsequent to it seems to be saying that (1) before the Supreme Being there was a time when nothing existed and that (2) after the Supreme Being there will be a time when nothing will exist. Consequently, when nothing existed, the Supreme Being did not exist; and when nothing will exist, the Supreme Being will not exist. So if when nothing already existed the Supreme Being did not yet exist, and if the Supreme Being will no longer exist when nothing will still exist, how is it that the Supreme Being did not begin to exist from nothing, or how is it that it will not come to nothing? What, then, did such an array of arguments accomplish if nothing so easily destroys their efficacy? For if it be established that the Supreme Being is subsequent to nothing, which precedes it, and ceases prior to nothing, which succeeds it, then all that necessary truth determined above is destroyed through a mere nothing. Or must this *nothing* be opposed, lest so many necessary structures of reason be overthrown by nothing and lest the Supreme Good, which has been sought-after and found by the light of truth, should be lost for nothing ?

Therefore, if possible, let us deny the proposition "Nothing existed before and will exist after the Supreme Being" rather than, while giving place to nothing before and after the Supreme Being, to reduce to nothing through nothing this Being, which through itself brought into existence what had been nothing. For the one expression – viz., "Nothing existed before the Supreme Being" – has a twofold meaning. For one sense of it is that before the Supreme Being existed there was a time when nothing existed; but the other meaning of it is: it is not the case that there was something before the Supreme Being. Similarly, if I were to say "Nothing taught me to fly," I might construe this [statement to mean] that *nothing itself* (in the sense of *not-anything*) taught me to fly – which would be false. Or [I might construe it to mean] that it is not the case that something taught me to fly – which is true.[39] And so from the first interpretation follows the inconsistency discussed above; and this interpretation must be rejected as in every respect false. But the second interpretation is perfectly consistent with earlier conclusions and is of necessity true in conjunction with them. Therefore, when it is said that nothing existed before the Supreme Being, the statement must be taken in the second sense. It must not be construed to mean that there was a time when nothing existed and the Supreme Being did not exist; rather, it must be construed to mean that it is not the case that there was anything before the Supreme Being. The same kind of twofold meaning occurs if we say that nothing will exist after the Supreme Being. Accordingly, if we examine carefully the interpretation which has been given concerning the word "nothing," then we conclude very truly that neither something nor nothing either preceded or will succeed the Supreme Being, and that nothing was before and will be after the Supreme Being. And nevertheless, the stability of our previously established conclusions is not shaken by a mere nothing.

Chapter Twenty: The Supreme Being exists in every place
and at all times.

It was concluded above[40] that this Creative Nature exists everywhere, in all things and through all things; and the fact that it
neither began to be nor will cease to be entailed that it always
was, is, and will be.[41] In spite of these conclusions I detect a
murmur of contradiction which compels me to investigate more
closely where and when the Supreme Being exists. Accordingly,
the Supreme Being exists either (1) always and everywhere or
(2) only in some place and at some time or (3) never and nowhere
– in other words, either (1) in every place and at every time or
(2) only in a limited place and for a limited time or (3) in no place
and at no time.

But what is more obviously objectionable than supposing that
what exists supremely and most truly, exists never and nowhere?
Therefore, it is false that the Supreme Being exists never or
nowhere. Moreover, without this Being there would exist neither
any good nor anything at all. Hence, if it existed never or nowhere, there would never or nowhere be anything good and
never or nowhere be anything at all. (It is not necessary to discuss
how false this consequence is.) (∼3) So it is false that the Supreme Being never and nowhere exists. Hence, it must exist only
in a limited place and for a limited time or else everywhere and
always. Assume that it exists only in a limited place and for a
limited time. Then, only where and when it existed could anything exist; where and when it did not exist, no being could
exist – because without the Supreme Being there would be
nothing. Thus, it would follow that there is a place and a time
at which there would not be anything at all existing. But this
consequence is false; for that time and that place would be
something. (∼2) Therefore, the Supreme Nature cannot exist
only in a limited place or for a limited time. Now, if it be said
that through itself this Nature exists only in a limited place or for
a limited time but that through its power it exists wherever and
whenever something is – this statement would not be true. For
since, clearly, this Nature's power is nothing other than itself,
its power exists in no way apart from itself. (1) Therefore, since

this Nature does not exist only in a limited place or for a limited time, it is necessary that it exist everywhere and always, i.e., in every place and at every time.

Chapter Twenty-one: [The Supreme Being] exists in no place
at no time.

But if the above conclusion holds, then either [the Supreme Being] exists as a whole in every place and at every time or else only a part of it [occupies all space and time], with the result that the rest of it exists outside of space and time.[42] But if it partly were and partly were not in every place and at every time, then it would have parts – a consequence which is false. Hence, it is not the case that only a part of it exists everywhere and always. But how is it as a whole everywhere and always? We must understand this either (1) in such way that the whole of it once occupies all space and time through its parts which are present in the different places and at the different times, or else (2) in such way that it exists as a whole even in each different place and at each different time. But if through its parts it is present in different places at different times, this Nature would not escape composition and division into parts – something which we have found to be totally foreign to the Supreme Nature. Hence, it does not exist as a whole in all places or at all times in such way that its parts are in different places and at different times. So the second alternative remains to be discussed, viz., how the Supreme Nature exists as a whole in every different place and at every different time. Now, without doubt, the Supreme Nature can be in these places or at these times only at the same time or else at different times. But since the law of space and the law of time (which hitherto one procedure was able to examine, since they moved forward together on the same track) here diverge from each other and seem to shun (as it were) debate by [taking] different routes, let each be examined separately in a discussion of its own. So first let it be seen whether the Supreme Nature can exist in different *places* as a whole – either at the same time or at different times. Then, let the same question be posed about different *times* [viz., the question whether at different *times* the Supreme Nature can exist as a whole – either at different times at once or else at different times successively].

If, then, the Supreme Nature were to exist as a whole in different *places* at once, these wholes would be different in the different places. For just as one place is distinct from another, so that they are different places – so what exists as a whole in one place is distinct from what at the same time exists as a whole in another place, so that they are different wholes. For none of what exists as a whole in a given place fails to exist in that place. And if none of a thing fails to exist in a given place, none of it exists at the same time anywhere besides in that place. Therefore, none of what exists wholly in a given place exists at the same time outside that place. But if none of it exists outside a given place, none of it exists at the same time in some other place. Thus, whatever exists as a whole in any place does not at all exist at the same time in another place. Accordingly, with regard to whatever exists as a whole in some place, how could it likewise exist as a whole in another place at the same time – if none of it can exist in another place? Therefore, inasmuch as one whole cannot at the same time exist as a whole in different places, it follows that in the different places there would be different wholes – if in different places there were something existing as a whole at the same time. Thus, if the Supreme Nature were to exist as a whole in every different place at the same time, there would be as many different supreme natures as there can be different places – a conclusion which it is unreasonable to believe. Therefore, it is not the case that the Supreme Nature exists as a whole in different places at the same time.

On the other hand, if [the Supreme Nature] were to exist as a whole in different places at different times, then while it existed in one place no good and no being would be present in other places because without the Supreme Being not anything at all exists. But these very places, which are something rather than nothing, prove this alternative to be absurd. Thus, it is not the case that the Supreme Nature exists as a whole in different places at different times.

But if it does not exist in different places as a whole either at the same time or at different times, clearly it does not at all exist as a whole in each different place.

I must now investigate whether this Supreme Nature exists as a whole at different *times* – either [existing at different times] at once or else [existing at different times] successively. But how could anything exist as a whole at different times at once, if these different times are not simultaneous? On the other hand, if this Nature were to exist as a whole distinctly and successively at different times (as a man exists as a whole yesterday, today, and tomorrow), then this Nature would properly be said to have existed, to exist, and to be going to exist. Therefore, its lifetime – which is nothing other than its eternity – would not exist as a whole at once but would be extended by parts throughout the parts of time. Now, its eternity is nothing other than itself. Hence, the Supreme Being would be divided into parts according to the divisions of time. For if its lifetime were produced through the process of time, it would together with time have a past, a present, and a future. But what is its lifetime or its length of existing other than its eternity? Consequently, since its eternity is identical with its essence (as unhasty reasoning unassailably proved in the foregoing discussion),[43] if its eternity had a past, a present, and a future its essence would also have to have a past, a present, and a future. Now, what is past is not present or future; and what is present is not past or future; and what is future is not past or present. Therefore, if the Supreme Nature were to exist at different times and to have temporal parts, how would what was previously demonstrated[44] by clear and rational necessity remain firm – viz., that the Supreme Nature is in no way composite but is supremely simple and supremely immutable? Or rather, if those conclusions are true [viz., that the Supreme Nature is supremely simple and immutable] – indeed, since they are clear truths – how are these conclusions possible [viz., that the Supreme Nature exists at different times and has temporal parts]? Hence, neither the Creative Being, its lifetime, nor its eternity admits in any way of a past or a future. (But if this Being truly [i.e., really] is, how could it fail to have a [timeless] present?) Yet to say that it was and that it will be is to signify a past and a future. Therefore, it never was and never will be. Consequently, it no more exists as a whole at different times successively than it exists as a whole at different times at once.

If, then, (as I have argued), the Supreme Being ($\sim$I) does not exist as a whole everywhere and always in such way that the whole of it once occupies all space and time through its parts, which are present in different places and at different times, and [if it (∼2) does] not [exist everywhere and always] in such way that it exists as a whole in each different place and at each different time, then clearly the Supreme Nature does not at all exist as a whole in every place and at every time. And since I have shown likewise that the Supreme Nature does not exist in every place or at every time in such way that part of it occupies all space and time while part of it is beyond all space and time, *it is impossible that* [the Supreme Nature] *exist everywhere and always*. For it could not at all be thought to exist everywhere and always except as a whole or as a part. Now, if it does not at all exist everywhere and always, it must exist either in a limited place and for a limited time or else in no place and at no time. But I have already proved[45] that it cannot exist in a limited place or for a limited time. Therefore, it must exist in no place and at no time, i.e., nowhere and never; for it could not exist except either in every place and at every time or else at a limited place and for a limited time.

On the other hand, since it has been uncontestably proven[46] not only (1) that the Supreme Nature exists through itself without beginning and end but also (2) that if it did not exist nothing would ever exist anywhere, *it is necessary that the Supreme Nature exist everywhere and always.*

Chapter Twenty-two: How [the Supreme Being] exists in every place at every time and in no place at no time.

How, then, will these two conclusions – so contradictory according to their utterance, so necessary according to their proof – be rendered consistent with each other? Well, perhaps the Supreme Nature does exist in space and time in a way which does not prevent it from so existing as a whole in different places at once and as a whole at different times at once that, nonetheless, it is not many wholes but only one, and that its lifetime (which is only its true eternity) is not divided into a past, a present, and a future. For only those things which exist in space and time in such way that they do not transcend spatial extension or temporal duration are bound by the law of space and time. Therefore, just as for things which do not transcend space and time it is said in all truth that one and the same whole cannot exist as a whole in different places at once and cannot exist as a whole at different times at once, so for those things which do transcend space and time the above statement need not hold true. For the following statements are seen to be correct: "A thing has a place only if a place contains the thing's size by delimiting it and delimits the thing's size by containing it"; and "A thing has a time only if a time somehow limits the thing's duration by measuring it and measures the thing's duration by limiting it." Therefore, if something's size or duration has no spatial or temporal limitation, then no place or time is truly ascribed to it. For since place does not affect it in the way that place does affect things, and since time does not affect it in the way that time does affect things, we may reasonably say that no place is its place and that no time is its time. But what is seen to have no place or time is shown clearly to be not at all subject to the law of space or time. Therefore, no law of space or time in any way restricts a nature which space and time do not confine by any limitation.

But which rational reflection does not exclude, on every account, the possibility that some spatial or temporal restriction confines the Creative and Supreme Substance, which must be different from, and free from, the nature and the law of all things which it created from nothing? For indeed, much rather, the Supreme Substance's power (which is identical with its essence) confines, by containing under itself, all the things which it made. How is it not also a mark of shameless ignorance to say that space delimits the greatness (*quantitatem*) – or that time measures the duration – of the Supreme Truth, which does not at all undergo increase or decrease of spatial or temporal extension?

Therefore it is a determining condition of space and time that only whatever is bounded by their limits cannot escape division into parts – whether the kind of division that its place undergoes according to its size or the kind of division that its time undergoes according to its duration. Nor can this thing in any way be contained as a whole in different places at once, nor as a whole at different times at once. (But whatever is not at all restricted by the restraints of space and time is not restricted by the law of space and time regarding the number of its parts, and is not prevented from being present as a whole at the same time in many places or times.) Since this, I say, is a determining condition of space and time, without doubt the Supreme Substance, which is not bound by the restraints of space and time, is not bound by the law of space and time. Therefore, since an inescapable necessity demands that the Supreme Being be present as a whole in every place and at every time, and since no law of space or time prohibits the Supreme Being from being present as a whole in every place at once or from being present as a whole at every time at once, the Supreme Being must be present as a whole in every different place at once and present as a whole at every different time at once. Its being present at one place or time does not prevent it from being simultaneously and similarly present at another place or time. Nor does the fact that it was or is or will be mean that something of its eternity (*a*) vanishes from the temporal present along with the past, which no longer exists, or (*b*) fades with the present, which scarcely exists, or (*c*) is going to come with the future, which does not yet exist. For the law of space and time does not in any way compel to exist or not to exist in any place or at any time (and does not in any way prevent from existing or not existing in any place or at any time) that which does not in any way confine its own existence within space and time. For if the Supreme Being is said to be in space or time, then even though on account of our customary way of speaking this one expression applies both to the Supreme Being and to spatial and temporal natures, nonetheless on account of the dissimilarity of these beings the meaning of the expression is different in the two cases. In the case of spatial and temporal natures the expression signifies two things: (1) that they are present in the places and at the times they are said to be present; and (2) that these natures are contained by these places and times. By contrast, in the case of the Supreme Being only one thing is understood, viz., that the Supreme Being is present – not, in addition, that it is contained.[47]

Therefore, if our ordinary way of speaking were to permit, it would seem more appropriate to say that [the Supreme Being] is *with* a place or a time than to say that it is *in* a place or a time. For saying that a thing is *in* another signifies that it is contained – more than does saying that a thing is *with* another. Therefore, [the Supreme Being] is not properly said to be *in* any space or time, because the Supreme Being is not at all contained by anything else. And yet, in its own way, it can be said to be in every place and time, inasmuch as all other existing things are sustained by its presence in order that they not fall away into nothing. [The Supreme Being] is in every place and time because it is absent from none; and it is in no place or time because it has no place or time. It does not receive into itself distinctions of space and time – as, for example, *here* or *there* or *somewhere*, or *now* or *then* or *sometime*. Nor does it exist in the fleeting temporal present which we experience, nor did it exist in the past, nor will it exist in the future. For these are distinguishing properties of finite and mutable things; but it is neither finite nor mutable. Nevertheless, these temporal modes can in a sense be predicated of the Supreme Being, inasmuch as it is present to all finite and mutable things just as if it were delimited by the same places [as they] and were changed during the same times [as they]. And so we see clearly (as clearly as is necessary for resolving what sounded contradictory) how according to the consistent truth of two different meanings the Supreme Being exists everywhere and always, nowhere and never – i.e., in every place and time, and in no place and time.

Chapter Twenty-three: How [the Supreme Being] can better be understood to be everywhere than in every place.

But since, demonstrably,[48] the Supreme Nature is not any more in all places than in all existing things (in them not as what is contained but as what contains all things by its pervasive presence), why is this Nature not said to be everywhere in the sense that it is understood to be in all existing things rather than [being understood to be] merely in all places? For the truth of the matter exhibits this understanding, and the propriety of spatial discourse does not at all preclude it. For it is our irreproachable practice often to predicate spatial terms of things which neither are places nor are contained by spatial limits. For example, I might say that the intellect[49] is *there* in the soul *where* rationality is. Now, although "there" and "where" are spatial terms, nonetheless the soul does not contain something within spatial limits, nor is the intellect or rationality contained. Therefore, according to the truth of the matter, the Supreme Nature is more appropriately said to be everywhere in the sense that it is in all existing things than merely in the sense that it is in all places. And it is necessary that the Supreme Nature exist in all existing things in such way that one and the same whole is completely and at once in every different thing – since (as the reasons presented earlier teach) the matter cannot be otherwise.

Chapter Twenty-four: How [the Supreme Being] can better be understood to exist always than to exist at every time.

It has also been established[50] that (1) the Supreme Substance is without beginning and without end and (2) that it does not have a past, a future, or a temporal (i.e., a fleeting) present such as we experience; for its lifetime, or eternity, which is identical with itself, is immutable and without parts. Consequently, if the word "always" – which seems to indicate time as a whole – is predicated of the Supreme Being, is not this term understood to signify eternity (which is never unlike itself) more truly than [it is understood to signify] temporal modalities (which in some respect are always unlike one another)? Hence, if the Supreme Being is said always to exist, then since for it to exist is the same as for it to live, nothing better is understood [by "always exist-ing"] than eternally existing, or eternally living – i.e., having an unending life which at once is completely whole. For its eternity is seen to be an unending life existing as a complete whole at once.[51] I have already proved[52] adequately that the Supreme Substance is nothing other than its own life and its own eternity, in no respect having boundaries, and existing only as a complete whole at once. Hence, what else is true eternity, befitting the Supreme Being alone, other than unending life existing as a complete whole at once? For by the fact alone that true eternity is present only in the Supreme Substance (which was proved to be the Creator and the only thing uncreated) we see clearly that true eternity is understood to be unlimited by a beginning and an end. But that this [temporal unlimitedness] does not befit any of the created things is demonstrated by the fact that they have been created from nothing.

Chapter Twenty-five: [The Supreme Being] is not mutable in
virtue of any accidents.

But is not the Supreme Being – which was clearly demonstrated[53] to be in every respect substantially identical with itself – ever at least accidentally different from itself? Yet, how is it supremely immutable if it can (I will not say *be* but) even be *thought to be* changeable through accidents? On the other hand, how can it fail to participate in an accident since it apparently *happens* to be greater than all other natures and unlike them?

But why would natural immutability be inconsistent with a susceptibility to certain traits which are called accidents – provided that no change in substance follows from the acquisition of these accidents?[54] Indeed, of all the things which are called accidents some (e.g., all colors) are understood to be able to be present or absent only in conjunction with some change in their participating subject. Others (e.g., certain relations) are known to cause, by their coming and going, no change at all in that object to which they are ascribed. For it is true that I am neither taller nor shorter than, equal nor similar to, a man who will be born after the present year. But after he is born, I will surely be able to have and to lose all of these relations to him – according as he will grow or change in various of his qualities – without any change in myself. So it is evident that of those traits which are called accidents, some bring change to some extent, whereas others do not at all diminish immutability.

Therefore, just as the Supreme Nature never in its simplicity admits of accidents which cause any change, so it does sometimes admit of being characterized by those predicates which do not at all oppose its supreme immutability. And yet, there does not *happen* to its being anything in terms of which the Supreme Nature can be regarded as mutable. Hence, we can also conclude that [this Nature] does not admit of any accident. Indeed, just as those accidents which cause some change as they come and go are regarded as really happening by their own effect, to the thing which they change, so those properties which do not have any such effect are found to be called accidents improperly. Therefore, just as the [Supreme Being] is always in every respect substantially identical to itself, so it is never in any respect even accidentally different from itself. But whatever may be the proper analysis of the word "accidents," it is certainly true that no term implying change can be predicated of the supremely immutable Nature.

Chapter Twenty-six: In what sense [the Supreme Being] is to be called substance. It is beyond every substance. It is uniquely whatever it is.

But if what has been seen about the simplicity of the Supreme Nature is right, how can the Supreme Nature be a substance? For although every substance is capable of being a mixture of differences or capable of changing its accidents, the immutable integrity of the Supreme Nature does not at all admit of any mixture or change. How, then, shall one maintain that it is some kind of substance – unless "substance" stands for "being," and so [this Nature] is both outside of and above every substance? Now, the Being which through itself is whatever it is and which makes from nothing every other being is different from that being which through another and from nothing is made whatever it is. As different as this one Being is from the other, so different is the Supreme Substance from those things which are not identical to it. And since of all natures this one alone has from itself, without the aid of another nature, its being whatever it is, how could it fail to be uniquely whatever it is and to have nothing in common with its creature? Hence, if it ever has some name in common with others, without doubt a very different signification must be understood [in its case].

Chapter Twenty-seven: Although [the Supreme Being] is not included in the usual classification of substances, it is a substance and an individual spirit.

Therefore, it is evident that this Substance, from which every other nature is excluded from having anything essentially in common, is not included in the usual classification of substances. To be sure, every substance is classified either as a universal, which is essentially common to many substances (as to-be-a-man is common to individual men), or else as a particular (*individua*), which has a universal essence in common with other particulars (as individual men have in common the fact that they are men). So how could anyone understand the Supreme Nature to be contained in the same classification as other substances? For neither is it common to many substances, nor does it have anything essentially in common with any other substance.[55] Nevertheless, since it not only most certainly exists but even exists supremely, and since the being of any thing is usually called substance, surely if [the Supreme Being] can be acceptably called anything, there is no reason not to call it a substance. And since no more excellent being is known than spirit or body – and of these two spirit is more excellent than body – certainly the Supreme Being must be called spirit, not body. However, since this Spirit has no parts, and since there cannot be more than one of these spirits, necessarily [this Spirit] is an altogether individual spirit.[56] For as shown previously,[57] [this Spirit] is not composed of parts, nor can it be understood to be changeable by any differences or accidents. Therefore, it is impossible for it to be divided in any way.

Chapter Twenty-eight: This Spirit exists in an unqualified sense; compared to it created things do not exist.

Therefore, from the foregoing considerations it is seen to follow that this Spirit, which exists in such a marvellously unique and uniquely marvellous way of its own, in a certain sense alone exists – while by comparison to it other things, whatever they are seen to be, do not exist.[58] For if we take a close look, only this Spirit will be seen to exist in an unqualified sense and completely and absolutely; and everything else will be seen almost not to exist and scarcely to exist. On account of its immutable eternity this Spirit can be said unqualifiedly to exist; it cannot be said, in accordance with some alteration, to have existed or to be going to exist. Nor is it, through being changeable, anything which at some time it was not or will not be; nor does it fail to be something which it once was or will be. Rather, whatever it is it is once, at once, and without limitation. Since, I say, it is this kind of being,[59] it is rightly said to exist in an unqualified sense and absolutely and completely.

Through being changeable, all other things in some respect at some time either were or will be what they now are not, or else they now are what at some time they were not or will not be. Moreover, what they were no longer exists; what they will be does not yet exist; and what they are in the fleeting, momentary, and scarcely existing present hardly exists. Therefore, since these things exist so changeably, they are justifiably denied to exist in an unqualified sense and completely and absolutely, and are asserted to exist scarcely at all and almost not to exist. Finally, all things other than this Spirit come from not-being into being through another instead of through themselves; and with respect to their own power, they would return from being to not-being unless they were sustained through another. Therefore, how could it befit them to exist in an unqualified sense or completely or absolutely instead of scarcely existing or almost not existing?

The existence of this sole ineffable Spirit can in no way be understood either to have begun from not-being or to be able to undergo any falling away (from that which it is) into not-being; moreover, whatever this Spirit is it is through no other than through itself – i.e., through that which it itself is. Therefore, is not its existence alone justifiably understood to be simple, complete, and absolute? But surely what exists so unqualifiedly and what alone is in every respect complete, simple, and absolute can in a certain respect rightly be said alone to exist. On the other hand, surely whatever through the above reasoning is known not to exist in an unqualified sense and completely and absolutely, but to exist scarcely at all or almost not to exist, is in a certain respect rightly said not to exist. So according to this reasoning the sole Creating Spirit exists, and all created things do not exist. Nevertheless, created things do not altogether lack existence, since from nothing they have been made something through this Spirit, which alone exists absolutely.

Chapter Twenty-nine: This Spirit's Expression is the very same thing as this Spirit. Nevertheless, there are not two spirits but only one.

But having examined these topics which up to now occurred to me (as I was following the guidance of reason) concerning the properties of the Supreme Nature, I now think it appropriate to consider, as best I can, the Supreme Nature's Expression, through which all things were made. For although all the points which I was able to notice earlier[60] concerning this Expression possess the inflexible strength of reason, the fact that this Expression is proved to be the same thing that the Supreme Spirit is compels me to discuss this Expression the more carefully. For if the Supreme Spirit made all other things only through itself, and if whatever was made by it was made through its Expression, how is this Expression anything other than what the Supreme Spirit is? Moreover, those truths which have already been discovered[61] declare uncontestably that nothing at all was ever able or is ever able to exist except for the Creating Spirit and its creatures. Now, it is impossible that the Expression of this Spirit should be in the class of created things; for every existing creature was created through this Expression – which could not have been created through itself. Indeed, nothing can be created through itself, because whatever is made exists later than that through which it is made, and because nothing exists later than itself. Thus, the other alternative holds, viz., that the Expression of the Supreme Spirit – since it cannot be a creature – is identical with the Supreme Spirit.

In short, this Expression can be understood to be nothing other than the understanding (*intelligentia*) of the Supreme Spirit by which the Supreme Spirit understands all things. For what else is it for this Spirit to speak a thing (in this way of speaking) than for it to understand it? For unlike a man, the Supreme Spirit never fails to express what it understands.[62] Therefore, if the supremely simple Nature is identical with what its understanding is – just as it is identical with what its wisdom is – then, necessarily, it is also identical with what its Expression is. But since I have already shown[63] that the Supreme Spirit is only singular and is in every respect an individual,[64] necessarily its Expression is so consubstantial with it that there is one Spirit rather than two.

Chapter Thirty: This Expression does not consist of many words, but is one word.

Why, then, should I continue to doubt what I earlier[65] left in doubt, viz., whether this Expression is many words or only one? For if [the Expression of the Supreme Nature] is so consubstantial with it that there is one Spirit rather than two, then surely just as the Supreme Nature is supremely simple, so too is this Expression. Therefore, it is not many words but is one word, through which all things have been made.[66]

Chapter Thirty-one: This Word is not the likeness of created things but is true Existence (*veritas essentiae*). Created things are a likeness of this true Existence. Which natures are greater and more excellent than others.

But, lo, a difficult question seems to me to arise – a question not to be left in any ambiguity. For all such words by which we mentally speak of objects (i.e., by which we think them) are likenesses and images of those objects for which they are words.[67] And every likeness and image is true in proportion to the exactness with which it imitates the thing whose likeness it is. What, then, must we believe about the Word by which all things were spoken and through which all things were made? Will it or will it not be the likeness of those things which were made through it? (1) If it is a true likeness of those mutable things, then it is not consubstantial with the Supreme Immutability – a consequence which is false. (2) On the other hand, if it is not in every respect a true likeness of mutable things but is a likeness [only] in some respects, then the Supreme Truth's Word is not altogether true – a consequence which is absurd. (3) Or if it has no likeness to mutable things, how were they made according to its form (*exemplum*)?

But perhaps no ambiguity will remain if [we make use of the following comparison]. The living man is said to be the true man (*veritas hominis*); but the likeness, or image, of a true man is said to be in a portrait of this man. By comparison, the Word is understood to be true Existence (*veritas existendi*); for the being of the Word exists so supremely that, in a way, it alone exists.[68] But a kind of likeness of this Supreme Being is understood to be in those things which in a way, by comparison with it, do not exist – even though they have been made something through it and in accordance with it. Thus, Supreme Truth's Word, which Word is itself the Supreme Truth, will not become something greater or something lesser by virtue of a greater or lesser degree of likeness to creatures. Rather, it must be the case that every created thing both exists and is excellent in proportion to its likeness to what exists supremely and is supremely great. For this reason, perhaps – or rather not perhaps but certainly – every intellect judges that living natures excel non-living natures in some way, and that sentient natures excel non-sentient natures, and that rational natures excel non-rational ones. For since the Supreme Nature in its own unique way not only exists but lives and experiences and reasons, clearly whatever existing thing in some respect lives is more like the Supreme Nature than what does not at all live. And what in some way (be it even by a bodily sense) recognizes an object [is more like the Supreme Nature] than what does not at all perceive. And what is rational [is] more [like the Supreme Nature] than what has no rational capacity. By a similar consideration it is clear that some natures exist more than others or less than others. For just as that is naturally more excellent which, with respect to its natural being, more closely approximates what is most excellent, so indeed that nature exists more whose being is more like the Supreme Being.[69]

I think that this same point can also be readily seen by means of the following consideration. From some substance which lives, perceives, and reasons let us imaginatively (*cogitatione*) remove first what is rational, next what is sentient, then what is vital, and finally the remaining bare existence. Now, who would not understand that this substance, thus destroyed step by step, is gradually reduced to less and less existence – and, in the end, to non-existence? Yet those characteristics which when removed one at a time reduce a being to less and less existence increase its existence more and more when added to it again in reverse order. Therefore, it is clear that a living substance exists more than does a non-living one, that a sentient substance exists more than does a non-sentient one, and that a rational substance exists more than does a non-rational one. So without doubt every being exists more and is more excellent to the extent that it is more like that Being which exists supremely and is supremely excellent. Thus, it is quite obvious that in the Word, through which all things were created, there is no likeness of created things but is, rather, true and simple Existence – whereas in created things there is not simple and absolute existence but a meager imitation of this true Existence. Hence, it must be the case that this Word is not more or less true according to a likeness to created things, but rather that every created nature consists of a higher degree of existence and excellence to the extent that it is seen to approximate this Word.

Chapter Thirty-two: The Supreme Spirit speaks itself by means of a coeternal Word.

Accordingly, how can what is simple Truth be the Word [or Image][70] of those things whose likeness it is not? For every word by which an object is thus mentally spoken is a likeness of that object. And if this Word is not a word [or image] of these things created through itself, then how can it really be a word? Without doubt, every word [or image] is a word [or image] of some thing;[71] accordingly, had there never been a creature, there would have been no word [or image] of a creature. What then? Must one conclude that if no creature in any respect existed, then the Word, which is the Supreme Being, in need of no other, would not at all exist? Or are we to think, perhaps, that the Supreme Being, which the Word is, would indeed be an eternal being but would not be a word if nothing had ever been created through it? For there can be no word [or image] of that which neither was, is, nor will be. But according to this reasoning,[72] if there had never existed any being except the Supreme Spirit, there would not have been a word in this Spirit. And if no word were in this Spirit, this Spirit would not speak with itself. And if it did not speak with itself, then it would not understand anything – since for it in this way to speak something is for it to understand something. And if it understood nothing then Supreme Wisdom, which is identical with this Spirit, would understand nothing – an utterly absurd consequence. What [follows], then? For if the [Supreme Spirit] were to understand nothing, how could it be Supreme Wisdom?

Or again, if there in no way existed anything other than Supreme Wisdom, what would this Wisdom understand? Would it [in that case] fail to understand itself? No, for how can we even think that Supreme Wisdom ever fails to understand itself, since a rational [human] mind can remember[73] not only itself but also the Supreme Wisdom, and can understand itself and the Supreme Wisdom? (For if the human mind could not have remembrance and understanding either of itself or of the Supreme Wisdom, then it would not be able – by debating silently with itself, just as my mind is now doing – to distinguish itself from irrational creatures and to distinguish the Supreme Wisdom from all its creatures.) Hence, just as the Supreme Spirit is eternal, so it eternally remembers and understands itself similarly to the way the rational mind remembers and understands itself. Or better, it remembers and understands itself according to no likeness but rather principally; and the rational mind [remembers and understands itself] in a way similar to this Spirit's [remembering and understanding itself]. But if the Supreme Spirit understands itself eternally, it speaks itself eternally. And if it speaks itself eternally, its Word is eternally with it. Consequently, whether this Spirit be thought of as not having any creatures or whether it be thought of as having creatures, its coeternal Word must be with it.

Chapter Thirty-three: The Supreme Spirit speaks both itself and its creation by means of one word.

But, lo, as I was inquiring just now about the Word by which the Creator speaks all that it created, I was confronted with the Word by which the Creator of all things speaks itself. Does the Creator, then, speak itself by means of one word and speak its creation by means of another? Or does the Creator by means of

the same word by which it speaks itself speak whatever it creates ?
For, necessarily, the Word by which the Creator speaks itself is
what the Creator is, just as is evident in the case of the Word by
which the Creator speaks the things created by it.[74] Even if
nothing were ever to exist except the Supreme Spirit, reason
would necessitate [as we have just seen] the conclusion that the
Word by which this Spirit speaks itself cannot fail to exist.
Consequently, what is more true than that the Word [or Image]
of this Spirit[75] is not anything other than what this Spirit is ?
Hence, if by a Word consubstantial with itself this Spirit speaks
itself and those things which it creates, then clearly the substance of the Word by which this Spirit speaks itself is one with
the substance of the Word by which it speaks creatures. So,
then, if there is only one substance, how could there be two
words ? On the other hand, perhaps the identity of substance
does not require us to admit a unity of word. For this Spirit,
which speaks by means of these words, has the same substance
as they do; but nevertheless this Spirit is not a word.

Certainly the Word by which Supreme Wisdom speaks itself
can most appropriately, according to the above reasoning, be
called the Word [or Image] of this Wisdom; for it has a perfect
likeness to this Wisdom. We cannot at all deny that when a
rational mind understands itself by thinking itself, a mental
image of the mind is produced – or better, the mind's thought of
itself is its own image, formed according to the likeness of the
mind and formed, as it were, from an impression of the mind.
The mind tries, as best it can, to formulate – either through
sensory imagination or through reason – the mental likeness of
whatever things it desires to think truly. The more truly it formu-
lates this likeness, the more truly it thinks that object. This
fact is noticed more clearly in cases where the mind thinks something other than itself – especially when it thinks of a material
object. For when in his absence I think of a man whom I know,
the sharpness of my thought is focused on that kind of image
of him which I contracted into my memory through the vision
of my eyes. This mental image is a word [or likeness] of this man
whom I speak of by thinking of him. Therefore, when a rational
mind understands itself by thinking of itself, it has an image of
itself begotten from itself – i.e., it has a thought of itself, formed
after the likeness of itself and formed from its own impression of

itself, as it were. Yet, only through its reason can a mind distinguish itself from its own image. And this image of the mind is a word [or likeness] of the mind.

So who would deny that in this way Supreme Wisdom begets its own consubstantial likeness, i.e., its Word, when it understands itself by speaking itself? Although nothing can properly or appropriately enough be said of a thing so uniquely excellent, nevertheless the Word can (not inappropriately) be called the image (*imago*), figure (*figura*), and form (*caracter*)[76] – as well as the likeness (*similitudo*) – of the Supreme Wisdom. Yet, this Word, by which Supreme Wisdom speaks creatures, is not at all likewise a word [or image] of creatures – because this Word is not the likeness of creatures but is rather the principal Existence. Thus, it follows that Supreme Wisdom does not speak creatures by a word [or image] of creatures. By what word, then, does it speak creatures if it does not speak them by a word [or image] of creatures? For that which Supreme Wisdom speaks, it speaks by a word; and a word is a word – i.e., a likeness – of something. But if Supreme Wisdom speaks nothing other than either itself or its creatures, then it can only speak either by the Word [or Image] of itself or else by a word [or image] of creatures. Therefore, if it does not speak anything by a word [or image] of creatures, then whatever it speaks it speaks by its own Word. Consequently, by one and the same Word it speaks itself and whatever it has created.

Chapter Thirty-four: How [the Supreme Spirit] can be seen to speak creatures by its own Word.

But how can such different things, viz., the Creating Being and the created being, be spoken by one word? – especially since this Word is coeternal with the speaker, whereas the created world is not. Perhaps when the Supreme Spirit speaks itself it speaks all created things *because* it itself is the Supreme Wisdom and Supreme Reason in which all created things exist (just as an object which is made according to the designing principles of some craft exists always – i.e., not only upon being made, but even before being made and after having perished – in these principles, as identical with what they are).[77] For before [created

things] were made and once they have been made and after they
have perished or have changed in some manner, they always
are in this Spirit what this Spirit is, rather than what they are in
themselves.[78] For in themselves they are a mutable being,
created according to immutable Reason. But in this Spirit they
are the primary Being and the primary true Existence; and the
more created things [in themselves] are in any way like this true
Existence, the more truly and excellently they exist. And so in
this way one can, not unreasonably, maintain that when the
Supreme Spirit speaks itself, it also speaks by one and the same
Word whatever has been created.

Chapter Thirty-five: Whatever was created exists as life and
truth in the Word and knowledge of the
Supreme Spirit.

But since it has been proved that the Word [or Image] of the
Supreme Spirit is consubstantial with it and perfectly similar to
it, necessarily all things existing in this Spirit exist also, in the
same way, in its Word. Therefore, whatever was created –
whether it lives or does not live, or however it exists in itself –
exists as life itself and truth itself in the Supreme Spirit.[79] But
since for the Supreme Spirit to know is for it to understand or
to speak, all that it knows it must know in the same way in which
it speaks or understands. Therefore, just as all things exist as
life and truth in the Word of this Spirit, so they [also] exist [as
life and truth] in this Spirit's knowledge.

Chapter Thirty-six: In what an incomprehensible manner the
Supreme Spirit speaks and knows the
things made by it.

From the foregoing can be most clearly comprehended that
human knowledge cannot comprehend how the Supreme Spirit
speaks and knows created things. For no one doubts that created
substances exist in themselves much differently from the way
they exist in our knowledge. In themselves they exist in virtue of
their own being; but in our knowledge their likenesses exist, not

their own being. It follows, then, that the more truly they exist anywhere by virtue of their own being than by virtue of their likenesses, the more truly they exist in themselves than in our knowledge. Now, it is certain that the more truly the Creating Being exists than does created being, the more truly every created substance exists in the Word (i.e., in the understanding) of the Creator than in itself. Therefore, how could the human mind comprehend what that kind of speaking and knowledge is which is so vastly superior to and truer than created substances, if our knowledge is as vastly surpassed by these created things as their likenesses are different from their being?

Chapter Thirty-seven: Whatever the Supreme Spirit is in relation to creatures this Spirit's Word also is. Nevertheless, both together are not more than one.

Since, plainly, the above arguments teach that the Supreme Spirit created all things through its own Word, did not its Word also create these same things? For since the Word is consubstantial with that of which it is the Word [or Image], the Word must be the Supreme Being. But the Supreme Being is only one being, which is the sole Creator and only Beginning of all created things. It alone, through no other than through itself, created all things from nothing. Wherefore, whatever the Supreme Spirit creates, its Word also creates in the same way;[80] and so whatever the Supreme Spirit is in relation to creatures its Word also in every respect is. And yet, both together are not more than one, for there are not many creating and supreme beings. Thus, just as this Spirit is the Creator and the Beginning of [all] things, so also is its Word. And yet they are not two, but are one Creator and one Beginning.

Chapter Thirty-eight: It cannot be said what two they are, although they must be two.

Thus, we must carefully give heed to something which, though very uncommon in the case of created things, is seen to hold true of the Supreme Spirit and its Word. Assuredly, whatever they are essentially and whatever they are in relation to creatures is present to each individually and to both together in such a way that it is wholly in each of the two without being more than one. For although this Spirit is itself completely the Creator and the Supreme Truth, and although its Word is also itself completely the Creator and the Supreme Truth, nevertheless both together are not two truths or two creators. But even though these observations are correct, still in a remarkable way it is perfectly clear that the Supreme Spirit, of which there is a Word [or Image], cannot be its own word; nor can the Word be this Spirit, of which it is the Word [or Image]. Thus, with respect to signifying what this Spirit and its Word are substantively and what they are in relation to creatures, they are always an individual unity. But with respect to the fact that the Supreme Spirit is not of the Word but that the Word is of the Supreme Spirit, they are an ineffable plurality. To be sure ineffable – because although necessity compels that they be two, what two they are cannot at all be expressed.[81] For even if in relation to each other they could possibly be called two equals, or some such thing, still if we ask regarding these relational terms "What is that of which they are predicated ?" we cannot answer in the plural – as we can when we are talking about two equal *lines* or two similar *men*. Indeed, they are not two equal spirits or two equal creators or two of anything which signifies either their essence or their relation to creatures. Nor are they two of anything which designates their relations to each other, for there are not two words or two images. For the Word, with respect to the fact that it is a word or an image, is related to the Supreme Spirit only in that it is the Word or Image of this Spirit; and being a word or image is so proper to the Word that this same characterization does not at all fit the Supreme Spirit. For this Spirit, of which there is a Word or Image, is itself neither word nor image. Therefore, it is certain that there cannot be expressed what two the Supreme Spirit and its Word are, even though it is necessary that they be two because of certain distinguishing properties which each has. For it is the distinguishing property of the one to be from the other; and it is the distinguishing property of the other that this one be from it.

Chapter Thirty-nine: This Word exists from the Supreme
Spirit by being begotten.

There surely seems to be no more fitting way to put this matter
than to say that it is the distinguishing property of the one to be
begotten from the other, and is the property of the other that this
one be begotten from it. For surely I have already proved[82]
that the Word of the Supreme Spirit does not exist from the
Supreme Spirit in the same way as do the things created by the
Supreme Spirit. Rather, it exists as Creator from Creator, as
the Supreme from the Supreme. Or, to sum up the full likeness
in a few words: The same thing exists altogether from the same
thing, and in such way that it does not at all exist except from
this thing. Therefore, since it is clear that (1) the Word of the
Supreme Spirit exists from it alone, in such way as to possess
its perfect likeness – as of offspring to parent – and since (2)
the Word does not exist from the Supreme Spirit as something
created by it, surely in no way can the Word more suitably be
thought to exist from the Supreme Spirit than by being begotten. Indeed, countless items are said, without qualm, to be
begotten from those things to which they owe their existence.
[We speak this way] even in cases where things do not, analogously to a child and its parent, resemble that from which they
are said to be begotten. For example, we say that hair is begotten
from a head and fruit from a tree, even though hair does not
resemble a head nor fruit a tree. If, then, many such things are
sensibly said to be begotten, then the more perfectly the Word
of the Supreme Spirit resembles the Supreme Spirit, like offspring to parent, by existing from it, the more fittingly the Word
can be said to exist from the Supreme Spirit by being begotten.

Chapter Forty: The Spirit is most truly parent, and the Word
most truly offspring.

But if the Word is most appropriately said to be begotten, and
if it is so like the Supreme Spirit from whom it is begotten, then
why should we think that the Word is *like* an offspring to its
parent? Why should we not rather maintain that the more

the Supreme Spirit alone suffices for effecting the Word's begottenness and the more the Word expresses the Supreme Spirit's likeness, the more truly the Supreme Spirit *is* a parent and the Word an offspring. For with regard to other things which are assuredly related as offspring to parent, none begets in such way that he alone needs no one else, but is completely sufficient by himself to beget offspring; and none is begotten in such way that he has no dissimilarity interspersed, but instead resembles his parent in every respect. Therefore, if the Word of the Supreme Spirit exists so entirely from this Spirit's essence alone, and resembles this Spirit so uniquely that no offspring exists as completely only from the essence of its parent or resembles its parent as much, surely the relationship of offspring to parent is seen to fit nothing more appropriately than the Supreme Spirit and its Word. Hence, the Supreme Spirit has the distinguishing property of being most truly a parent, and the Word has the distinguishing property of being most truly an offspring.

Chapter Forty-one: The Supreme Spirit most truly begets
and the Word is most truly begotten.

But this conclusion [above] will not be able to stand unless, in equal degree, (1) the Supreme Spirit most truly begets and (2) the Word is most truly begotten. Therefore, just as the first is clearly true, so must the second be completely certain. Hence, it is the distinguishing property of the Supreme Spirit most truly to beget and the property of the Word most truly to be begotten.

Chapter Forty-two: It is the property of the one to be most
truly begetter and father; and it is the
property of the other to be most truly
begotten and son.

I should now like to infer, if I can, that the Supreme Spirit is most truly father and the Word most truly son. Yet, I think I ought not to by-pass the question of which set of terms is more suitable for them – "father and son" or "mother and daughter" – for there is no sexual distinction in the Supreme Spirit and the Word. For if the Supreme Spirit is appropriately father and its offspring appropriately son because each is spirit, then by parity of reasoning why is it not appropriate for the one to be mother and the other to be daughter because each is truth and wisdom?[83] Is it [preferable to call them father and son] because among those natures which have a difference of sex it is characteristic of the better sex to be father or son and of the inferior sex to be mother or daughter? Now, although such is naturally the case for many beings, for others the reverse holds true. For example, in some species of birds the female sex is always larger and stronger, the male sex smaller and weaker.

But surely, the Supreme Spirit is more suitably called father than mother because the first and principal cause of offspring is always in the father. For if the paternal cause always in some way precedes the maternal cause, then it is exceedingly inappropriate for the name "mother" to be applied to that parent whom no other cause either joins or precedes for the begetting of offspring. Therefore, it is most true that the Supreme Spirit is father of its own offspring. But if a son is always more like a father than is a daughter, and if no one thing is more like another than this offspring is like the Supreme Father, it is most true that this offspring is a son, not a daughter. Therefore, just as this Spirit has the distinguishing property of most truly begetting and this offspring of most truly being begotten, so the former has the distinguishing property of being most truly the begetter and the latter of being most truly the begotten. And just as the one is most truly a parent and the other most truly an offspring, so the one is most truly a father and the other most truly a son.

Chapter Forty-three: Reconsideration of what is common to both and of what is proper to each.

Now that we have discovered so many and such important properties of each[84] – properties by which a certain remarkable plurality, as ineffable as it is necessary, is proved to exist in the Supreme Unity, I find it especially delightful to reflect more frequently on such an impenetrable mystery (*secretum*). For, lo, it is so impossible for the one who begets and the one who is begotten to be the same, and so impossible for the parent and the offspring to be the same, that it is necessary for the Begetter to be other than the Begotten and for the Father to be other than the Son. And yet, it is so necessary for the one begetting to be the same as the one begotten and for the parent to be the same as the offspring that it is impossible for the Begetter to be other than what the Begotten is or for the Father to be other than what the Son is. Although both exist in such way that the fact of their being two is perfectly clear, nonetheless what either of them is is so one and the same as what the other is that what two they are is thoroughly hidden.[85] For the Father and the Son are so different that when I speak of both I see that I have spoken of two; yet what the Father and the Son are is so identical that I do not understand what I have called two. For although the Father considered by Himself is completely the Supreme Spirit and the Son considered by Himself is completely the Supreme Spirit, nevertheless the Spirit-as-father and the Spirit-as-son are so one and the same that the Father and the Son are not two spirits but one. Thus, just as the properties which are unique to each do not admit of plurality because they do not characterize both, so what is common to both constitutes an individual unity even though it exists as a whole in each. For just as there are not two fathers or two sons but only one father and one son since the properties of the Father are different from the distinguishing properties of the Son, so there are not two spirits but only one even though it is true of both Father and Son that each is completely spirit. The Father and the Son are so opposite in relation that the one never sustains the distinguishing property of the other; and they are so concordant in nature that the one always has the essence of the other. For with respect to the fact that the one is the Father and the other is the Son they are so different that the Father is never called the Son nor the Son called the Father; and with respect to their substance they are so identical that the essence of the Son is always in the Father and the essence of the Father is always in the Son. For their essence is the same rather than different, one rather than many.

Chapter Forty-four: How the one is the essence of the other.

Thus, to say that the one is the essence of the other involves no departure from the truth; rather it suggests the supreme unity and supreme simplicity of a common nature. For there is a difference between the way in which a wise man is wise through wisdom and cannot be wise through himself, and the way in which the Father is the essence (*essentia*) of the Son and the Son the essence of the Father. For it is not the case that the Son is existent through the Father and the Father through the Son in such way that the one could not be existent except through the other – just as a man cannot be wise except through wisdom.[86] For just as Supreme Wisdom is always wise through itself, so the Supreme Being always exists through itself. But the Father is completely the Supreme Being, and the Son is completely the Supreme Being. Therefore, the Father exists completely through Himself and likewise the Son exists completely through Himself – even as each is wise through Himself. For the Son is not less perfect existence (*essentia*) or wisdom because He is existence begotten from the existence of the Father and wisdom begotten from the wisdom of the Father. But the Son *would* be less perfect existence or wisdom if He did not exist through Himself or were not wise through Himself. Yet, there is no inconsistency at all involved in the Son's existing through Himself and having existence from the Father. For the Father has existence, wisdom, and life in Himself, so that He exists through His own being, is wise through His own wisdom, and lives through His own life (rather than through another's being, wisdom, or life). Similarly, by begetting [the Son] he bestows on Him the having of existence, wisdom, and life in Himself [i.e., in the Son Himself], so that the Son exists through His own being, is wise through His own wisdom, and lives through His own life (rather than through another's being, wisdom, or life).[87] Otherwise, the existence (*esse*) of the Father and of the Son would not be identical, nor would the Son be equal to the Father. But we have already seen[88] most clearly how false this consequence is.

So, then, the fact that the Son exists from the Father is not inconsistent with the fact that the Son exists through Himself. For it is necessary that He have from the Father the very ability to exist through Himself. If some wise man were to teach me his wisdom which previously I lacked, surely his wisdom would not improperly be said to do this [i.e., to cause my wisdom]. But although my wisdom would owe its existence and its being-wise to his wisdom, nevertheless once my wisdom existed it would exist only by its own being and would be wise by itself only. Therefore, it is all the more true that the eternal Father's co-eternal Son – who has existence from the Father in such way that they are not two beings – exists, is wise, and lives through Himself. Therefore, "The Father is the essence of the Son" or "The Son is the essence of the Father" cannot be understood as if the one were [able to exist] through the other but not able to exist through Himself. Rather, in order to signify their commonness of supremely simple and supremely singular essence, it can be fittingly said and understood that the one so is the very same thing as the other that the one has the essence of the other. And so, on the basis of the fact that for either of them to have an essence is simply to be an essence, just as the one has the essence of the other, so the one is the essence of the other – i.e., the one has the same being (*esse*) as the other.

Chapter Forty-five: The Son can more fittingly be called the essence of the Father than the Father [can be called the essence] of the Son. Similarly, the Son is the strength of the Father, the wisdom of the Father, and the like.

Although according to the aforeseen reasoning this last conclusion is true, nevertheless for the Son to be called the essence of the Father is much more appropriate than for the Father to be called the essence of the Son. For since the Father has His essence from no one except Himself, He is not very appropriately said to have anyone's essence except His own. But because the Son has His essence from the Father and because He has the same essence as the Father has, the Son can very suitably be said to have the Father's essence. Therefore, since neither the Father nor the Son has an essence otherwise than by being an essence:

just as the Son is much more fittingly understood to have the Father's essence than the Father to have the Son's essence, so the Son can more appropriately be said to be the essence of the Father than the Father can be said to be the essence of the Son. For in making this one utterance we indicate tersely that the Son not only has the same essence as the Father but also that He has this essence from the Father. Thus, to say that the Son is the essence of the Father is to say that the Son is not a different essence from the essence of the Father – or better, is not different from the Father-essence. Similarly, therefore, the Son is the Father's strength, wisdom, truth, justice, and whatever else befits the essence of the Supreme Spirit.

Chapter Forty-six: How various of the statements expressed
above can also be understood in another way.

Nevertheless, various statements which can be thus expressed and understood are seen to admit also of another meaning which is not inconsistent with the present construal. For clearly the Son is the true Word – i.e., the perfect understanding, cognition, knowledge, and wisdom of the whole paternal substance. That is, the Son understands, cognizes, knows, and comprehends the essence of the Father. Therefore, if the Son is called the understanding, wisdom, knowledge, and cognition, or conception, of the Father in the sense that He understands, comprehends, knows, and cognizes the Father – there is no departure at all from the truth. Moreover, the Son can very fittingly be called the truth of the Father – not only in the sense that the truth of the Son is identical with the truth of the Father (as we have already seen),[89] but also in the sense that in the Son there is understood to be (not an imperfect image of the paternal substance but) the whole truth of the paternal substance, for He is the same as what the Father is [i.e., the same essence].

Chapter Forty-seven: The Son is understanding of
understanding, truth of truth, etc.

But if the substance of the Father is understanding, knowledge, wisdom, and truth, it follows that as the Son is the understanding, knowledge, wisdom, and truth of the paternal substance, so He is understanding of understanding, knowledge of knowledge, wisdom of wisdom, truth of truth.

Chapter Forty-eight: The Father is referred to as memory, just as the Son is referred to as understanding. How the Son is the understanding (or wisdom) of memory, the memory of the Father, and memory of memory.

But what are we to believe about memory? Ought the Son to be thought to be the understanding of memory, or the memory of the Father, or the memory of memory? Indeed, since we cannot deny that Supreme Wisdom remembers[90] itself, nothing is more fitting than that just as the Son is referred to as the Word, so the Father is referred to as memory – for the word seems to be born from memory, as we observe more clearly in regard to our own minds. For since the human mind does not always think of itself (as it does always remember itself), it is clear that when it thinks of itself the word [or image] of itself is begotten from memory. Apparently, then, if the mind were always to think of itself, the word [or image] of itself would always be born from memory. For to think of a thing which we remember is to speak this thing mentally; but this thought formed from memory and formed in the thing's likeness is the word [or image] of the thing. Hence, concerning the Supreme Wisdom, which always speaks itself as well as always remembering itself, we can see clearly that the coeternal Word is begotten from the eternal memory. Therefore, as the Word is fittingly understood to be an offspring, so memory is very aptly called a parent. Hence, if an offspring begotten completely from the Supreme Spirit alone is an offspring of this Spirit's memory, nothing follows more consistently than that the Supreme Spirit is its own memory. Indeed, with respect to the Supreme Spirit's remembering itself, the Supreme Spirit is not in its own memory as one thing is in another – as is the case with those remembrances which exist in the human mind's memory in such way that they are not our memory itself. Rather, this Spirit remembers itself in such

way that it is its memory of itself. Hence, it follows that as the
Son is the understanding and wisdom of the Father, so He is the
understanding and wisdom of the paternal memory. Now, whatever the Son comprehends or understands, He likewise remembers. Therefore, the Son is the memory of the Father and the
memory of memory (i.e., memory remembering the Father, who
is memory), as He is also the wisdom of the Father and the wisdom of wisdom (i.e., wisdom comprehending the Father, who is
wisdom). And, indeed, the Son is memory begotten from
memory – just as He is wisdom begotten from wisdom. But the
Father is memory and wisdom begotten from no other.

Chapter Forty-nine: The Supreme Spirit loves itself.

But, lo, as I am contemplating with delight the distinguishing
properties of the Father and the Son, together with what they
have in common, I find in the Father and the Son nothing more
delightful to reflect upon than the affection of mutual love. For
how absurd it would be to deny that the Supreme Spirit loves
itself as well as remembering and understanding itself – since
even a rational [human] mind, from the fact that it can remember
and understand both itself and this Spirit, is proved to be able
to love both itself and this Spirit. For the remembrance and
understanding of any thing whatsoever is in vain and is altogether useless except that this thing be loved or condemned
to the extent that reason requires. Therefore, the Supreme
Spirit loves itself, just as it also remembers and understands
itself.

Chapter Fifty: This love proceeds equally from the Father
and the Son.

To one who is rational it is surely clear that the Supreme Spirit
does not remember itself and understand itself because it loves
itself but rather loves itself because it remembers itself and
understands itself. Clearly, moreover, this Spirit cannot love
itself unless it remembers itself or understands itself. For
nothing is loved without being remembered or understood,

62

whereas many things are remembered and understood without being loved. So, clearly, the Supreme Spirit's love proceeds from its remembering and understanding itself. But if the Father is referred to as the memory of the Supreme Spirit, and if the Son is referred to as the understanding of the Supreme Spirit, then it is obvious that the love of the Supreme Spirit proceeds equally from the Father and the Son.[91]

Chapter Fifty-one: The Father and the Son love themselves and each other in equal degree.

But if the Supreme Spirit loves itself, then without doubt the Father loves Himself, the Son loves Himself, and the Father and the Son love each other. For the Father considered by Himself is the Supreme Spirit, and the Son considered by Himself is the Supreme Spirit, and both together are one spirit. Moreover, [they love themselves and each other] because each remembers and understands both Himself and the other in an equal degree. And since what loves and what is loved is wholly the same for the Father and for the Son, it is necessarily the case that each loves Himself and the other in an equal degree.

Chapter Fifty-two: This Love is as great as the Supreme Spirit.

How great, then, is the Supreme Spirit's love – a love so mutual to the Father and the Son? If the Supreme Spirit loves itself to the extent that it remembers and understands itself, and if it remembers and understands itself in proportion to its essence – as cannot fail to be the case – then surely the Supreme Spirit's Love is as great as this Spirit itself.

Chapter Fifty-three: This Love is the same thing that the Supreme Spirit is; and yet, this Love is one spirit with the Father and the Son.

But what can be equal to the Supreme Spirit except the Supreme Spirit? Hence, this Love is the Supreme Spirit. In fact, if there never had been a creature – i.e., if nothing had ever existed other than the Supreme Spirit, who is Father and Son – nonetheless, the Father and the Son would still have loved themselves and each other. Hence, it follows that this Love is identical with what the Father and the Son are, viz., the Supreme Being. Now, since there cannot be many supreme beings, what is more necessary than that the Father, the Son, and their Love be one Supreme Being? Therefore, this Love is the Supreme Wisdom, the Supreme Truth, the Supreme Good, and whatever else can be predicated of the substance of the Supreme Spirit.

Chapter Fifty-four: [This Love] proceeds as a whole from the Father and as a whole from the Son. Nevertheless there is only one love.

We must consider closely whether there are (1) two loves – one proceeding from the Father and the other proceeding from the Son – or (2) one love proceeding not as a whole from either one but proceeding partly from the Father and partly from the Son or (3) neither two loves nor one love which proceeds partly from the Father and partly from the Son but rather one and the same love proceeding as a whole from each distinctly and as a whole from both together. Now, the solution to this question is unquestionably recognized from the following consideration: The Supreme Spirit's Love does not proceed from the Father and the Son with respect to the fact that they are two but with respect to the fact that they are one. For the Father and the Son equally send forth such a great good not from their relations, which are plural (the one relation is that of father, the other that of son), but from their essence, which does not admit of plurality.[92] Therefore, as the Father considered distinctly is the Supreme Spirit and the Son considered distinctly the Supreme Spirit, and yet the Father and the Son together are not two spirits but are one spirit, so the Supreme Spirit's Love proceeds as a whole from the Father considered distinctly and as a whole from the Son considered distinctly and as one and the same whole (not as two wholes) from the Father and the Son together.

Chapter Fifty-five: [This Love] is not the son of the Father
and of the Son.

What then? Since this Love has its existence equally from the
Father and the Son, and since it is so like them that it is in no
respect unlike them but is completely what they are, must it be
regarded as their son or their offspring? Now, as soon as con-
templated, the Word evidences most clearly, by manifesting the
clear image of its parent, that it is the offspring of the one from
whom it exists. By comparison, [the Supreme Spirit's] Love
clearly denies that it is an offspring, because when it is understood to proceed from the Father and the Son, it does not immediately exhibit, to one contemplating it, as clear a likeness to
the one from whom it exists – even though reflective reason
teaches that this Love is completely what the Father and the
Son are. Indeed, if this Love were the offspring of the Father
and the Son, one of the two would be the father of this Love and
the other would be the mother, or else both would be fathers or
else both would be mothers – three alternatives which are seen
to be contrary to the truth. On the one hand, since this Love
does not proceed at all differently from the Father than from the
Son, it is wrong[93] to refer to the Father and the Son differently
in relation to this Love; thus it is not the case that the one is its
father and the other its mother. On the other hand, there is no
precedent in nature for supposing that[94] there are two things
each of which has, equally, a perfect and exactly similar relation
of father or mother to some one thing. Thus, it is not the case
that both the Father and the Son are fathers or mothers of this
Love which proceeds from them. Therefore, that the Love of
the Father and the Son is their son or their offspring is seen not to
agree in any respect with the truth.

Chapter Fifty-six: Only the Father is begetter and unbegotten.
Only the Son is begotten. Only their Love
is neither begotten nor unbegotten.

But according to our practice in ordinary discourse, this Love (it
seems) cannot at all be called unbegotten; nor can it be called

begotten, as properly as can the Word. For we are accustomed frequently to say that a thing is begotten from that from which it exists. For example, we say that heat or brightness is begotten from fire, or that an effect is begotten from its cause. According to this reasoning, then, the Love which proceeds from the Supreme Spirit cannot without qualification be called unbegotten On the other hand, it cannot as properly be called begotten as can the Word. For clearly the Word is most truly an offspring and most truly a son; but clearly this Love is not at all a son or an offspring. Thus, only He of whom the Word [or Image] is, can – or rather, ought to – be called begetter and unbegotten; for He alone is father and parent, and in no way exists from another. And only the Word [should be called] begotten, since it alone is son and offspring. And only the Father and the Son's Love [should be called] neither begotten nor unbegotten, since (1) it is neither son nor offspring and (2) it does not altogether avoid existing from someone else.

Chapter Fifty-seven: This Love is uncreated and creator, even as are the Father and the Son. Nevertheless, they are together one uncreated creator, not three. This Love can be called the Spirit of the Father and the Son.

This Love considered distinctly is the Supreme Being, even as are the Father and the Son; and yet the Father and the Son and their Love are not many, but are one Supreme Being, which alone is uncreated by anyone else and which created all else only through itself. Therefore, we must infer that just as the Father considered distinctly is uncreated and creator, and as the Son considered distinctly is uncreated and creator, so their Love considered distinctly is uncreated and creator. Nevertheless, all three together are one uncreated creator and not three. Thus, no one makes or creates or begets the Father. And only the Father begets (but does not create) the Son. And the Father and the Son neither create nor beget their Love; but in some way – if it can be thus expressed – they equally breathe out their Love. For although the supremely immutable Being does not breathe as we do, still perhaps it cannot at all more fittingly be said to send from itself its own Love (which proceeds ineffably from it by existing from it rather than by parting from it) than by breathing.

Furthermore (if we may speak this way), as the Word of the Supreme Being is its son, so the Love of the Supreme Being can quite suitably be called its spirit.[95] Thus, although this Love is essentially spirit, even as the Father and the Son are essentially spirit, nevertheless the Father and the Son are not thought to be anyone's spirit – because the Father is not from anyone else, nor is the Son begotten from the Father's breathing Him out, as it were. Rather, this Love may be thought to be the spirit of the Father and of the Son because it marvellously proceeds from both, who breathe it out in a certain unique and ineffable way. Moreover, because this Love is common to the Father and the Son, it is reasonably regarded as able to take as its own a name which is common to the Father and the Son, should the need of a proper name require one. But indeed, if it happens that this Love is referred to by the proper name "Spirit" – a name which signifies the substance of the Father and the Son equally – then this occurrence will usefully serve to indicate that this Love is what the Father and the Son are, even though it has its own existence from them.

Chapter Fifty-eight: As the Son is the essence and wisdom of the Father in the sense that He has the same essence and wisdom as the Father, so their Spirit is the essence, wisdom, and the like, of the Father and the Son.

As the Son is the substance, wisdom, and strength of the Father in the sense that He has the same essence, wisdom, and strength as the Father, so their Spirit can also be understood to be the essence, wisdom, and strength of the Father and of the Son in that He has exactly the same essence, wisdom, and strength as they.

Chapter Fifty-nine: The Father and the Son and their Spirit exist equally in one another.

It is pleasing to contemplate how the Father, the Son, and their Spirit are present in one another with such equality that no one of them excels the other. For aside from the fact that each of them is so perfectly the Supreme Being that all three together are only one Supreme Being which cannot be separate from itself or outside itself, or greater-or-lesser than itself, this very same fact[96] can be proven with respect to each taken by Himself. For the Father as a whole is in the Son and in the Spirit common to Him and the Son; and the Son is in the Father and in this same Spirit; and this same Spirit is in the Father and in the Son. For the memory of the Supreme Being is present as a whole in its understanding and its love; and its understanding is present as a whole in its memory and in its love; and its love is present as a whole in its memory and its understanding. Indeed, the Supreme Spirit understands and loves the whole of its memory; and it remembers and loves the whole of its understanding; and it remembers and understands the whole of its love. But the Father is referred to as memory, the Son as understanding, and their Spirit as love. Therefore, the Father, the Son, and their Spirit so equally encompass one another and are so equally present in one another that no one of them can excel the other or exist without Him.

Chapter Sixty: No one of them needs the other for remembering, understanding, or loving – because each singly is memory, understanding, love, and whatever else must be present in the Supreme Being.

But in regard to these [three] I think that what occurs to me as I investigate must be carefully kept in mind. The Father must be so understood as memory, the Son as understanding, and the Spirit as love that the Father does not need either the Son or the spirit common to them, the Son does not need the Father or this same Spirit, and this Spirit does not need the Father or the Son.

We must not suppose that the Father can only remember through Himself, while being able to understand only through the Son and to love only through His and the Son's spirit; or that the Son can only understand through Himself, while remembering through the Father and loving through His own spirit; or that this same Spirit can only love through Himself, while the Father remembers for Him and the Son understands for Him. For each of these three singly is the Supreme Being and Supreme Wisdom so perfectly that this Being and Wisdom remembers, understands, and loves through itself. Consequently, none of these three could possibly need one of the others in order to remember or understand or love. For each singly is essentially memory, understanding, love, and whatever else must be present in the Supreme Being.

Chapter Sixty-one: Nevertheless, there are not three [fathers or three sons or three spirits] but one father, one son, and one spirit common to them.

I notice that at this point a question arises. For if the Father is understanding and love as well as memory, and if the Son is memory and love as well as understanding, and if their Spirit is memory and understanding as well as love (indeed, such was the manner in which we understood that the Father is memory, the Son understanding, and their Spirit love), then how can the Father avoid being a son and someone's spirit? And why is the Son not a father and someone's spirit? And why is their Spirit not someone's father and someone's son? Now, these questions are not difficult to answer provided we reflect upon the conclusions already discovered rationally. Although the Father is understanding and love, He is not a son or anyone's spirit, because He is not understanding as begotten from another or love as proceeding from another. Whatever He is He is only as one who begets and as one from whom another proceeds. Moreover, although the Son by Himself remembers and loves, He is not a father or anyone's spirit, because He is not memory which begets or love which proceeds from another in the way that His Spirit does. Whatever He is He is only as one begotten and as one from whom a spirit proceeds. Moreover, the fact that the Spirit is comprised of memory or understanding does not entail that He is a father or a son, because the Spirit is not memory which begets or understanding which is begotten. Rather, whatever He is only proceeds. Therefore, what prevents us from concluding that there is only one Father, one Son, and one Spirit in the Supreme Being – not three fathers or three sons or three spirits ?

Chapter Sixty-two: How from these [viz., the Father, the Son, and their Spirit] many sons seem to be begotten.

But let what I now see not perchance contradict this assertion [above]. For there ought to be no doubt that the Father and the Son and their Spirit each speaks of Himself and the other two (just as each also understands Himself and the other two). But if so, how is it that in the Supreme Being there are not as many words as there are ones speaking and being spoken of? For if several men utter one thing mentally, there seem to be as many words [or images] of this thing as there are thinkers, because a word [or image] of this thing is in each one's thought. Likewise, if one man thinks several things, there are as many words in his mind as there are things thought. But when a man thinks of something which is outside his mind, the word [or image] of the object thought of is not begotten from the object itself since the object itself is not present in the mental vision. Rather, the word is begotten from a likeness or an image of the object – either an image which is in the memory of the one thinking, or else possibly an image which, during the time that the person is perceiving, is conducted from the perceived object into the mind by means of the bodily senses. Yet, in the Supreme Being the Father and the Son and their Spirit are always so present to one another (for, as already noted,[97] each of them is no less present in the others than in Himself) that when they speak of one another, the one who is spoken of seems to beget His own word, just as when He speaks of Himself. Therefore, if each one of them begets His own word when He speaks of Himself or is spoken of by another, how is it that the Son, or how is it that the

Spirit of the Father and of the Son, fails to beget anything? Moreover, according to the above reasoning the Supreme Substance must beget as many sons and send forth as many spirits as there are words which can be proved to be begotten from it. Consequently, by this reasoning, not only do there seem to be in the Supreme Being many fathers and sons and processions but also many other relations.

Chapter Sixty-three: How in the Supreme Spirit there is only one son and one who has a son.[98]

On the other hand, surely the Father and the Son and their Spirit (all of whom, it is already most certain, really exist) are not three speakings – even though each, considered singly, speaks. Nor is more than one thing spoken of when each speaks of Himself and of the other two. For just as it belongs to the Supreme Wisdom to know and to understand, so it is surely the nature of eternal and immutable Knowledge and Understanding always to behold as present that which it knows and understands. Yet, for the Supreme Spirit to speak in such way is simply for it mentally to see, as it were – even as our own mental speaking is nothing other than a mental seeing. Now, reasons already considered[99] have made it most certain that whatever belongs to the Supreme Nature essentially, belongs also with perfect consistency to the Father distinctly, to the Son distinctly, and to their Spirit distinctly; and yet that very characteristic does not admit of plurality if it is predicated of the three together. Now, it has been established[100] that just as knowledge and understanding pertain to the essence of the Supreme Spirit, so knowing and understanding are for the Supreme Spirit the same as speaking – i.e., the same as always beholding as present – what it knows and understands. Consequently, it is necessary that just as the Father distinctly, the Son distinctly, and their Spirit distinctly, know and understand without being together three knowings or understandings but only one knowing and one understanding, so each one, considered distinctly, speaks without being together three speakings but only one. Hence, we can also recognize clearly that when these three [viz., the Father, the Son, and their Spirit] are spoken of – whether each speaks of Himself or whether they speak of one another – there are not many beings which are spoken of. For what is spoken of there except their essence ? Hence, if this essence is only singular, then what is spoken of is only singular. Thus, if what speaks is one in them, and if what is spoken of is one (for one wisdom speaks in them, and one substance is spoken of), necessarily there are not many words in the Supreme Spirit but only one word. Consequently, although each speaks of Himself and all speak of one another, still in the Supreme Being there cannot be any other word than the Word which (we have proven)[101] is so begotten from the one whose word it is that it can be called this one's true image and truly is His son.

In this fact I see something marvellous and inexplicable. For, lo, although it is clear that (1) the Father, the Son, and the Spirit of the Father and the Son each speaks equally of Himself and the other two, and that (2) there is only one word in the Supreme Spirit, nevertheless this Word cannot in any way, it seems, be called the word of all three but can only be called the word of one of them. For we have established[102] that the Word is the image and the son of the one whose word it is; and clearly it cannot appropriately be called the son or the image either of itself or of the spirit proceeding from it. For the Word is not begotten from itself, and is not begotten from the spirit which proceeds from it; nor does the Word through existing imitate either itself or the one proceeding from it. Indeed, the Word does not imitate itself or contract from itself the likeness of existing, because imitation and similarity require that there be at least two things [viz., the imitating and the imitated]. Nor does the Word imitate the proceeding Spirit, nor exist in His likeness – because the Son does not exist from the proceeding Spirit but rather the Spirit exists from the Son. Therefore, the alternative remains that this Word alone is [the word] only of Him from whom it has its existence by being begotten and in whose perfect likeness it exists. Therefore, in the Supreme Being there is one father, one son, and one proceeding spirit – rather than more than one father, son, or proceeding spirit. And these are so three that the Father is never the Son or the proceeding Spirit; nor is the Son ever the Father or the proceeding Spirit; nor is the Spirit of the Father and the Son ever the Father or the Son. Moreover, each [of these three], distinctly, is so complete that He needs no other. Nonetheless, what the three are is so one that just as it cannot be predicated plurally of each considered distinctly, so it cannot be predicated plurally of the three together. And although each of them speaks of Himself equally as all speak of one another, nevertheless there are not many words but only one. And this Word is [the word] not of each distinctly or of all together but of one of them alone.

Chapter Sixty-four: Although inexplicable, this [teaching] must be believed.

The hiddenness of so sublime a matter seems to me to surpass the utmost power of the human intellect; and so I think that I ought to refrain from attempting to explain how this doctrine is true. For I think that anyone who is investigating an incomprehensible doctrine should be content if by rational inference he comes to recognize that this doctrine is most certainly true – even if he is unable to comprehend how it could be true. Yet, even if because of their naturally deep incomprehensibility we cannot explain these doctrines which are supported by necessary proofs and opposed by no contradicting reason, we ought nonetheless to regard them with faith's certainty. But what is so incomprehensible, so ineffable, as that which is higher than all other things? Therefore, if the statements previously made about the Supreme Being have been asserted on the basis of necessary inferences (*necessariis rationibus*), then the firm certainty of these statements is not at all shaken, even though they cannot be comprehended to the point that they can be expressed in words.[103] For if our previous reflection rationally comprehends that it is incomprehensible how the Supreme Wisdom knows the things it created (about which things we inevitably know so much), who could explain how this Wisdom knows or speaks of itself (about which Wisdom either nothing or nearly nothing can be known by us)? Therefore, if by virtue of Supreme Wisdom's speaking of itself the Father generates and the Son is generated, "who shall explain His generation?"[104]

Chapter Sixty-five: How regarding this ineffable matter
something true was stated.

But on the other hand, if Supreme Wisdom is so ineffable[105] –
or rather, because it is so ineffable – how will there hold true
what was stated in regard to the relation of Father and of Son
and of proceeding Spirit? For if what was stated was explained
by sound (*vera*) reasoning, then how is the Supreme Wisdom
inexplicable? Or if it is inexplicable, how is what was stated
true? [Is not the case as follows?]: This Wisdom was to some
extent able to be explained, and so nothing precludes the truth
of what was stated; but because this Wisdom was not able to be
fully comprehended, it is ineffable. But what can be said about
that which was established in the preceding[106] discussion?: viz.,
that the Supreme Being is so above and outside every other
nature that whenever something is predicated of it in words
which are also applied to other natures, the sense of these words
is not at all the same in the two cases.[107] For in all those
words which I thought, did I understand any meaning except the
customary and ordinary meaning? So if the ordinary meaning
of these words does not apply to the Supreme Being, none of
my previous inferences apply to it. Therefore, how could it be
true that something was discovered about the Supreme Being
if what was discovered is far different from the Supreme Being?

What then? [Could it be that] in one respect something was
discovered about an incomprehensible being, whereas in another
respect nothing was discovered about it? For we often say many
things which we do not express precisely as they are.[108] Instead,
we signify obliquely (*per aliud*) that which we either cannot or
else do not want to express properly (e.g., when we speak in
riddles). And often we see a thing, though not properly (i.e.,
not as the object itself is) but rather by means of a likeness or an
image (e.g., when we see someone's face in a mirror). Thus,
we do and do not say one and the same thing; we do and do not
see one and the same object. We speak and see obliquely; we
do not speak and see in accordance with the respective reality.
So in this manner, if the Supreme Nature is not at all assumed
to be expressed in accordance with the reality of its essence but

74

is assumed to be somehow or other designated obliquely, then nothing precludes the truth of all that was earlier stated about the Supreme Nature, and nothing prevents this Nature from remaining as ineffable as ever. For whatever words seem to be predicable of this Nature do not so much reveal it to me in its reality as hint at it through a likeness.[109] For when I think the meanings of these words, I more readily conceive of what I observe in created things than of that Being which I know to transcend all human understanding. By their respective significations these words form in my mind something much less than – indeed, something far different from – that toward which my mind, by means of these inadequate meanings, tries to advance in order to understand. For the word "wisdom" does not suffice for disclosing to me this Being through which all things were created from nothing and are kept from [falling away into] nothing. Nor can the word "being" express that [reality] which is far above all things by virtue of its unique loftiness, and which is far removed from all things by virtue of its own nature. So, then, this Nature is ineffable because words cannot at all express it as it is; and yet, if under the instruction of reason we can apprehend something about it obliquely, as in a dark manner,[110] [this apprehension] is not false.

Chapter Sixty-six: Through the rational mind one comes nearest to knowing the Supreme Being.

Therefore, since it is evident that something about this Nature can be perceived not with respect to its reality but only obliquely (*per aliud*), it is certain that one more closely approaches a knowledge of it through that which more closely approximates it in likeness. For among created things whatever is shown to be more similar to the Supreme Nature must be more excellent by nature. Therefore, by virtue of its greater likeness [this created thing] more greatly aids the inquiring mind to approach the Supreme Truth, and by virtue of its more excellent created being it more fully teaches what the mind ought to believe about the Creator. Hence, without doubt the more the Creative Being is investigated by reference to a creature more near to itself, the more thoroughly this Being is known. For the argument

considered earlier[111] leaves no doubt that every being in the degree
to which it exists is in that degree similar to the Supreme Being.
Clearly, then, just as the rational mind alone of all creatures is
able to mount an investigation of the Supreme Being, so equally
the rational mind alone is that through which the rational mind
itself is most able to advance toward finding the Supreme Being.
For we already know[112] that the rational mind most nearly
approximates the Supreme Nature through a likeness of natural
being. Therefore, what is clearer than that (1) the more earnestly
the rational mind attends to studying itself, the more effectively
it ascends to knowledge of the Supreme Being, and (2) the more
it neglects inspecting itself, the more it wanes from contemplating the Supreme Being?

Chapter Sixty-seven: The mind is the mirror and image of the
Supreme Being.

The mind, then, can very appropriately be called its own mirror,
as it were, in which it beholds, so to speak, the image of this
Being which it cannot see face to face.[113] For if of all created
things the mind alone can remember itself,[114] understand, and
love, then I do not see why we should deny that there is in it the
true image of this Being, which exists as an ineffable trinity of
memory, understanding, and love. Indeed, by the fact that the
mind can remember, understand, and love the Supreme Being
it proves the more truly that it is the image of the Supreme
Being. For the greater the mind is and the more similar it is to the
Supreme Being, the truer image of the Supreme Being it is
known to be. Yet, there cannot at all be thought to have been
naturally bestowed upon the rational creature anything as excellent and as similar to the Supreme Wisdom as is the ability to
remember, to understand, and to love that which is the greatest
and best of all. Therefore, nothing else which so displays the
image of the Creator was bestowed upon any creature.

Chapter Sixty-eight: The rational creature was created for
loving the Supreme Being.

And so it seems to follow that the rational creature ought

earnestly to desire nothing as much as to express, as a voluntary effect, this image impressed on it as a natural ability. For aside from the rational creature's owing what he is to his Creator: from the fact that he is known to be able [to do] nothing as excellent as remembering, understanding, and loving the Supreme Good, he is proved without doubt to be under obligation to will nothing as principally [as the Supreme Good]. For who would deny that the better things over which we have power ought more to be willed?

In the last analysis, for a rational nature to be rational is nothing other than for it to be able to distinguish what is just from what is unjust, what is true from what is not true, what is good from what is not good, what is better from what is worse. But the ability to make these distinctions is thoroughly useless and superfluous to rational nature unless what it distinguishes it also loves or disapproves in accordance with the dictates of correct discrimination. Hence, we see very clearly that every rational being exists for the following purpose, viz., that even as by rational discrimination he judges a thing to be more or less good, or else to be no good at all, so he might love that thing in proportionately greater or lesser degree, or else reject it. Therefore, nothing is clearer than that the rational creature was made for this end, viz., to love above all other goods the Supreme Being, which is the Supreme Good. Or better, [he was made] so that he might love nothing except the Supreme Being or on account of the Supreme Being – since the Supreme Being is good through itself and nothing else is good except through it. Yet, the rational creature cannot love the Supreme Being without striving to remember and to understand it. Clearly, then, the rational creature ought to devote his entire ability and will to [the end of] remembering, understanding, and loving the Supreme Good – to which end he knows that he has his existence.

Chapter Sixty-nine: The soul which always loves the Supreme Being lives at some time in true happiness.

But without doubt the human soul is a rational creature. Hence it must have been made for the purpose of loving the Supreme

Being. Necessarily, then, it was made either so that it might love [this Being] endlessly or else so that it might at some time lose this love either freely or by force. But it is blasphemous to suppose that Supreme Wisdom created the soul so that the soul might sometime despise such a great good or else might lose it by force, while willing to keep it. Thus, the alternative remains that the soul was created for loving the Supreme Being endlessly. However, the soul cannot love endlessly unless it always lives. Consequently, it was created so that it might always live – provided it always wills to do that for which it was made. Moreover, it would be altogether unbefitting for the omnipotent, supremely good, and supremely wise Creator to cause not to exist, while it was truly loving Him, a thing which He created for the purpose of loving Him. And [it would be altogether unbefitting for Him] to remove or permit to be removed from a being which loved Him the gift which He freely gave to this being when it did not love Him so that it might always love Him – a removal which would necessitate this being's not loving Him. [This possibility seems] all the more [unsuitable] since we ought in no way to doubt that the Creator loves every nature which truly loves Him. Therefore, it is evident that the human soul's life will never be removed from it – provided it always earnestly desires to love the Supreme Life.

What kind of life, then, will the soul have? In fact, of what value is a long life unless it is truly free from distressful intrusions? For whoever during his lifetime is subject to distress either because of fear or suffering, or whoever is deceived because of a false security – how does he live except wretchedly? By contrast, anyone who lives free of these conditions lives happily. But it is thoroughly preposterous that a nature which always loves Him who is both omnipotent and supremely good would always live wretchedly. Clearly, then, the human soul is such that if it keeps that end for which it exists, it will at some time live happily – truly free from death itself and every other form of distress.

Chapter Seventy: The Supreme Being gives itself as a reward
to the soul which loves it.

Accordingly, we cannot at all regard as true the supposition that
the most just and most powerful Being gives no reward to a
soul loving it so persistently – a soul to which, not loving it, it
gave existence so that this soul could love it. For were this
Being to give no reward to a soul loving it, Supreme Justice
would not be distinguishing between *loving* what ought to be
loved supremely and *despising* what ought to be loved supremely.
Moreover, either Supreme Justice would not be loving a soul
which was loving it, or else to be loved by Supreme Justice
would be of no advantage. But these consequences are all
incompatible with Supreme Justice. Therefore, it rewards every
soul that perseveres in loving it.

But what does Supreme Justice give as a reward? If to what
was nothing it gave a rational being, so that this being would love
it, what will it give to a soul which loves it without ceasing to
love it? If the [initial] assistance to love is so great, how great is
the recompense to love? And if such is the supporting of love,
what will be the nature of love's gain? For if the rational creature, which without this love is useless to itself, is so eminent
among all creatures, surely nothing can be this love's reward
except what is preeminent among all natures. For the Supreme
Good, which thus demands to be loved, requires no less that it
be desired by the soul loving it. For who could love justice,
truth, happiness, and incorruptibility in such way as not to
desire to enjoy them? Therefore, with what shall supreme
Goodness reward the soul which loves and desires it if not with
itself?[115] For whatever else it bestows it does not bestow as a
reward, because [any other bestowal] would neither compensate
the love nor console the loving soul nor satisfy its desires.

On the other hand, if Supreme Goodness willed to be loved
and desired in order to give some other reward, then Supreme
Goodness would will to be loved and desired not for its own sake
but for the sake of something else. And so it would not will
to be loved but would will that this other thing be loved – a
blasphemous thing to suppose. Therefore, nothing is truer than

that every rational soul at some time shall receive the Supreme Beatitude to enjoy – provided the soul strives as it should to desire Supreme Beatitude out of love for it. As a result, what the soul now sees as if through a glass, darkly, it shall then see face to face.[116] But to question whether or not the rational soul will enjoy Supreme Beatitude endlessly would be very foolish. For while enjoying this Beatitude the soul cannot be tormented by fear or deceived by a false security. Nor having experienced the need of this Beatitude can the soul keep from loving it. Nor will Supreme Beatitude forsake a soul which loves it. Nor will there be anything more powerful which will separate it and the soul against their wills. Therefore, any soul which once begins to enjoy Supreme Beatitude will be eternally happy.

Chapter Seventy-one: The soul which despises the Supreme Being will be eternally wretched.

From these conclusions surely we can consistently infer that the soul which despises loving the Supreme Good will incur eternal wretchedness. Now, if someone were to say, "For such contempt the soul would be more justly punished by losing its existence, or life, since the soul does not use itself for that end for which it was made," then reason would not at all allow the supposition that the soul, after such great guilt, should be punished by becoming what it was before any guilt. Now, before the soul existed it was not able to have guilt or to be aware of punishment. Therefore, if after despising the end for which it was made the soul were so to die that it did not experience anything or so that it were absolutely nothing, its condition would be the same in the case of greatest guilt as in the case of no guilt; moreover, supremely wise Justice would not be discriminating between (1) what can [do] no good and wills no evil, and (2) what can [do] the greatest good but wills the greatest evil. But how unsuitable this consequence is is quite plain. So then, nothing can be seen to follow more consistently, and nothing ought to be believed more assuredly, than that man's soul was created in such way that if it despises loving the Supreme Being it will suffer eternal wretchedness. Consequently, just as the loving soul will rejoice in an eternal reward, so the despising soul will grieve in eternal punishment. And as the former will experience immutable sufficiency, so the latter will experience inconsolable need.

Chapter Seventy-two: Every human soul is immortal.

But if the soul were mortal, then the soul which loves [the Supreme Being] could not be eternally happy; nor could the soul which despises [the Supreme Being] be eternally wretched. Thus, whether the soul loves or despises that which it was created to love, necessarily the soul is immortal. Now, if there are rational souls which must be deemed to be neither loving nor despising – as the souls of infants seem to be – what must be believed about them? Are they mortal or immortal? Well, without doubt, all human souls are of the same nature. Therefore, since some have been proven to be immortal, every human soul must be immortal.

Chapter Seventy-three: The soul is either always wretched or else at some time truly happy.

But since any living thing either never is, or else at some time is, truly free from all troubles, it is no less necessary that every human soul be either always wretched or else at some time truly happy.

Chapter Seventy-four: No soul is unjustly deprived of the Supreme Good. The soul is supposed to seek the Supreme Good wholeheartedly.

I think that it is certainly either very difficult or else impossible for any mortal man to be able to ascertain by rational investigation (1) which souls are unhesitantly to be deemed as so loving the end which they were created to love that they deserve at some time to enjoy this end, (2) which souls so despise this end that they deserve always to be in need of it, and (3) in what manner or by what merit the souls which apparently can be called neither loving nor despising are assigned to eternal happiness or eternal misery. Nevertheless, we must most certainly maintain that the supremely just and supremely good Creator of things does not unjustly deprive any soul of that good for which it was created; moreover, every man is supposed to seek this same good by loving and desiring it with all his heart, all his soul, and all his mind.[117]

Chapter Seventy-five: We are to hope for the Supreme Being.

But the human soul would not at all be able to engage in this endeavor if it despaired of being able to attain what it was seeking. Therefore, the hope of attaining is as much necessary to the human soul as the desire for seeking is useful.

Chapter Seventy-six: We are to believe in the Supreme Being.

But that which does not believe cannot love or hope. Therefore, it is useful for the human soul to believe the Supreme Being and those things which are a necessary condition for loving it, so that the soul by believing may strive unto it. Yet, I think that this same idea can be conveyed suitably and more tersely if instead of saying "by believing, to strive unto the Supreme Being" we say simply "to believe in the Supreme Being." For if someone declares that he believes in the Supreme Being, he seems sufficiently enough to indicate [thereby] that (1) he strives for the Supreme Being through the faith which he is professing, and that (2) he believes those things which pertain to this striving. For someone who believes what does not pertain to striving unto the Supreme Being or who does not strive for the Supreme Being through what he believes does not seem to believe in the Supreme Being.

Probably it makes no difference whether we say "to believe *in* the Supreme Being" or "to believe *on* the Supreme Being" – just as we can accept as the same the expressions "by believing, to strive *unto* the Supreme Being" and "by believing, to strive *for* it."[118] Yet, whoever by striving unto it will arrive, will remain within it rather than remaining outside it; and this idea is more explicitly and more familiarly indicated by saying that [the soul] must "strive unto the Supreme Being" than by saying that [the soul] ought to "strive for the Supreme Being." And so for this reason I think that "[The soul] ought to believe *in* the Supreme Being" can be said more fittingly than "[The soul] ought to believe *on* the Supreme Being."

Chapter Seventy-seven: We ought to believe equally in the Father, the Son, and their Spirit – in each distinctly and in all three together.

Therefore, we ought to believe equally in the Father, the Son, and their Spirit – in each distinctly and in all three together. For the Father considered distinctly is the Supreme Being, the Son considered distinctly is the Supreme Being, and their Spirit considered distinctly is the Supreme Being; and the Father and the Son, together with their Spirit, are together one and the same Supreme Being in which alone every man ought to believe, since this is the singular end which each man out of love ought to strive unto in every thought and deed. Hence, it is evident that just as a man can strive unto the Supreme Being only if he believes in this Being, so believing therein is of no avail to anyone unless he strives thereunto.

Chapter Seventy-eight: Which faith is alive and which is dead.

Therefore, with whatever degree of certainty so important a matter is believed, this belief will be useless and as something dead unless it is made alive and strong by love. Yet, this faith, which its corresponding love accompanies, is not at all useless – provided the opportunity to use it arises. Rather this faith exercises itself in a great number of works – something which it could not do in the absence of love. These claims can be proven by the solitary fact that what loves Supreme Justice can neither despise anything just nor admit of anything unjust. Now, whatever accomplishes something shows thereby that it possesses the vital force without which it could not accomplish what it did. Consequently, we may without absurdity say that (1) working faith is alive because it has the vital force of love, without which it could not accomplish what it does, and that (2) idle faith is not alive because it lacks the vital force of love with which to accomplish anything. Thus, if we designate as *blind* not only someone who has lost his sight, but also someone who does not have sight and yet ought to have it, why can we not likewise call faith without love *dead* – not because it has lost its vital force (i.e., its love) but because it does not have the vital force which it ought always to have?[119] Therefore, just as faith which works through love[120] is recognized to be living faith, so faith which is idle through contemptuousness is shown to be dead. Thus, living faith can quite suitably be said to believe *in* what ought to be believed in, whereas dead faith can be said merely to believe what ought to be believed.

Chapter Seventy-nine: What three the Supreme Being can in some respect be said to be.

Lo, it is clearly advantageous for every man to believe in an ineffable Unity which is trine and Trinity which is one. Indeed, [this Being is] one and a unity by virtue of one essence; but I do not know by virtue of what three it is trine and a trinity. For although I can speak of a trinity because of the fact that the Father, the Son, and their Spirit are three, nevertheless I cannot in a single word name that by virtue of which they are three (as if I were to say "[a trinity] by virtue of being three *persons*," as I might say "a unity by virtue of being one *substance*"). For they must not be thought to be three persons, because in cases where there are more persons than one, all these persons exist independently of one another, so that there must be as many substances as there are persons – as we recognize in the case of men, who are as many individual substances as they are persons. Therefore, just as there are not many substances in the Supreme Being, so there are not many persons.

Thus, if someone should want to speak to someone else about the Trinity, what three will he say that the Father, the Son, and their Spirit are unless perhaps, compelled by the lack of a properly suitable word, he chooses a word from among those which cannot be predicated plurally of the Supreme Being [and uses this word] for signifying what cannot be said by a suitable word ? For instance, he might say that this wonderful Trinity is one being or nature and three *persons* or *substances*. For these last two words are quite fittingly selected for sigifying a plurality in the Supreme Being, since the word "person" is predicated only of an individual rational nature[121] and since the word "substance" is predicated mainly of individual things, which mostly exist in plurality. For individuals, especially, support accidents – i.e., are subject to accidents; and so individuals are quite properly called substances. (Accordingly, we have already seen[122] that the Supreme Being, which is subject to no accidents, cannot *properly* be called a substance – except where "substance" is a substitute for "being.") Therefore, on the basis of this rational necessity, the Supreme Trinity which is one, or Supreme Unity which is trine, can irreproachably be called one being and three *persons* or *substances*.

Chapter Eighty: The Supreme Being exercises dominion over all things and rules all things and is the only God.

Therefore, it seems – or rather, it is unhesitatingly affirmed – that this Being which we call God is not nothing and that the name "God" is properly assigned to this Supreme Being alone. Indeed, everyone who affirms that a God exists (whether one God or more than one) understands [thereby] nothing other than a Substance which he believes to be above every nature that is not God – a Substance which men are to worship because of its excellent worthiness and which they are to entreat against lurking misfortune. What, though, is so to be worshipped because of its worthiness and implored in regard to any matter whatsoever as is the supremely good and supremely powerful Spirit, which exercises dominion over all things and rules all things ? For just as we have established[123] that all things were created through, and are sustained by, this Spirit's supremely good and supremely wise omnipotence, so it would be altogether unsuitable to think that (1) this Spirit does not have dominion over what it created by itself, or that (2) the things created by it are ruled over by some other less powerful, less good, or less wise being, or that (3) they are directed by no rational principle at all but only by a random changing, due to chance occurrences. For this Spirit alone is the one through whom anything is well-off and without whom nothing is well-off and from whom, through whom, and in whom all things are. Therefore, since this Spirit alone is not only the good Creator but also both the most powerful Lord and the wisest Ruler of all, it alone (we see most clearly) is the one whom every other nature to its full ability ought to worship lovingly and love worshipfully. [And, most clearly, this Spirit is the one] from whom alone good fortune is to be hoped for, to whom alone flight from adversity is to be taken, and of whom alone supplication is to be made for anything whatsoever. Truly, then, this Spirit not only is God but is also the only God – ineffably three and one.

PROSLOGION

Preface

Upon the insistent adjurations of certain brothers I wrote a short work – as an example of meditating about the rational basis of faith – in the role of someone who by arguing with himself investigates what he does not yet know. Afterwards,[1] considering this work to be composed of a chain of many arguments, I began to ask myself whether perhaps a single argument could be found which would constitute an independent[2] proof and would suffice by itself to demonstrate that (1) God truly [really] exists, that (2) He is the Supreme Good, needing no one else yet needed by all else in order to exist and to fare well, and that (3) He is whatever else we believe about the Divine Substance. I often and earnestly turned my attention to this goal. At times what I was in quest of seemed to me to be apprehensible; at other times it completely eluded my mental powers. At last, despairing, I wanted to give up my pursuit of an argument which I supposed could not be found. But when I wanted to shut out the very thought [of such an argument], lest by engaging my mind in vain, it would keep me from other projects in which I could make headway – just then this argument began more and more to force itself insistently upon me, unwilling and resisting as I was. Then one day when I was tired as a result of vigorously resisting its entreaties, what I had despaired of finding appeared in my strife-torn mind in such way that I eagerly embraced the reasoning I had been anxiously warding off. Supposing, then, that to record what I had joyously discovered would please its readers, I wrote the following short work on this subject (and on various others) in the role of someone endeavoring to elevate his mind toward contemplating God and seeking to understand what he believes. And although I deemed neither this present writing nor the former one as worthy to be called a treatise or to bear the name of an author, nevertheless I thought that they should not be circulated without titles which in some way would issue to anyone coming across them an invitation to read them.

Hence, I gave a title to each – calling the first *An Example of Meditating about the Rational Basis of Faith* and calling the present work *Faith Seeking Understanding*.[3] But after a number of people had already copied both works under these respective titles, I was urged by several readers to prefix my name to these writings – urged especially by Hugh,[4] the reverend archbishop of Lyons and apostolic legate in Gaul, who on the basis of his apostolic authority directed me to do this. To make the affixing of my name less inappropriate, I retitled the first writing *Monologion*, i.e., a soliloquy, and the present writing *Proslogion*, i.e., an address.

Chapter One: Arousing the mind for contemplating God.

Come now, insignificant man, leave behind for a time your preoccupations; seclude yourself for a while from your disquieting thoughts. Turn aside now from heavy cares and disregard your wearisome tasks. Attend for a while to God and rest for a time in Him. Enter the inner chamber of your mind; shut out all else except God and whatever is of aid to you in seeking Him; after closing the chamber door, think upon your God.[5] Speak now, my whole heart; speak now to God: I seek Your countenance; Your countenance, O Lord, do I seek.[6] So come now, Lord my God, teach my heart where and how to seek You, where and how to find You. If You are not here, Lord, where shall I seek You in Your absence? But if You are everywhere, why do I not behold You in Your presence? Surely You dwell in light inaccessible.[7] Yet, where is this inaccessible light? Or how shall I approach unto a light inaccessible? Or who will lead me to and into this light so that in it I may behold You? Again, in what signs or appearances shall I seek You? Never have I seen You, O Lord my God; I am not acquainted with Your countenance. What shall this Your distant exile do? What shall he do, O most exalted Lord? What shall Your servant do, anguished out of love for You and cast far away from Your presence?[8] He pants to see You, but Your face is too far removed from him. He desires to approach You, but Your dwelling place is inaccessible. He desires to find You but does not know Your abode. He longs to seek for You but does not know Your countenance. O Lord, You are my God and my Lord; yet never have I seen You. You have created me and created me anew, and have bestowed upon me whatever goods I have; but not yet do I know You. Indeed, I was made for seeing You; but not yet have I done that for which I was made.

O the wretched fate of man when he lost that end for which he was made! O that hard and ominous fall! Alas, what he lost and what he found, what vanished and what remained! He lost the happiness for which he was created and found a wretchedness for which he was not created. The necessary condition for happiness vanished and the sufficient condition for wretchedness remained. Man then ate the bread of angels[9] for which he now hungers; and now he eats the bread of sorrows,[10] which then he did not know. Alas, the common mourning of all men, the universal lament of the sons of Adam! Adam burped with satiety; we sigh with hunger. He abounded; we go begging. He happily possessed and wretchedly deserted; we unhappily lack and wretchedly desire, while, alas, remaining empty. Why did he not, when easily able, keep for us that of which we have been so gravely deprived? Why did he shut us out from the light and enshroud us in darkness? Why did he take life away from us and inflict death? Wretched creatures that we are, expelled from that home, impelled to this one; cast down from that abode, sunken to this one! [We have been banished] from our homeland into exile, from the vision of God into our own blindness, from the delight of immortality into the bitterness and horror of death. O miserable transformation from such great good into such great evil! What a grievous loss, a heavy sorrow, an unmitigated plight!

But, alas, pitiable me, one of the miserable sons of Eve far removed from God – what did I set out to do; what have I achieved? Where was I heading; where have I arrived? To what was I aspiring; for what do I sigh? I sought after good things[11] and, behold, here is turmoil.[12] I was reaching out for God, but tripped over myself. I was seeking rest in solitude, but I found tribulation and grief[13] in my inmost self. I wanted to laugh with joy of mind, but am constrained to cry out in lamentation of heart.[14] I hoped for joy, but, lo, my sighs increase! O Lord, how long? How long, O Lord, will You forget us? How long will You turn away Your face from us?[15] When will You look upon us and hear us? When will You enlighten our eyes[16] and show us Your face?[17] When will You restore Yourself to us? Look upon us, O Lord, hear us, enlighten us, reveal Yourself unto us. Restore Yourself unto us so that it may go well with us for whom it goes so badly without You. Have compassion upon the efforts and attempts which we direct toward You, without whom we can do nothing. As You summon us, so aid us.[18] I beseech You, Lord, that I may not despair with sighing but may revive with hope. I implore You, Lord, to sweeten by Your consolation my heart made bitter by its own desolation. I adjure You, Lord, that having begun hungering to seek You, I may not finish without partaking of You. I set out famished; let me not return still unfed. I came as one who is poor to one who is rich, as one who is wretched to one who is merciful; let me not return empty and spurned. And if before I eat I sigh,[19] grant that at the end of my sighing I may have food to eat. O Lord, bent over as I am I can only look downwards; straighten me so that I can look upwards. Having mounted above my head, my iniquities cover me over; and as a heavy burden they weigh me down.[20] Deliver me from them, unburden me, so that the abyss of iniquities does not engulf me.[21] Permit me, at least from afar or from the deep, to look upwards toward Your light. Teach me to seek You, and reveal Yourself to me as I seek; for unless You instruct me I cannot seek You, and unless You reveal Yourself I cannot find You. Let me seek You in desiring You; let me desire You in seeking You. Let me find You in loving You; let me love You in finding You.

O Lord, I acknowledge and give thanks that You created in me Your image so that I may remember,[22] contemplate, and love You. But this image has been so effaced by the abrasion of transgressions, so hidden from sight by the dark billows of sin, that unless You renew and refashion it, it cannot do what it was created to do. Lord, I do not attempt to comprehend Your sublimity, because my intellect is not at all equal to such a task. But I yearn to understand some measure of Your truth, which my heart believes and loves. For I do not seek to understand in order to believe but I believe in order to understand. For I believe even this: that I shall not understand unless I believe.[23]

Chapter Two: God truly, [or really], exists.

Therefore, Lord, Giver of understanding to faith, grant me to understand – to the degree You deem best – that You exist, as we believe,[24] and that You are what we believe You to be. Indeed, we believe You to be something than which nothing greater can be thought. Is there, then, no such nature as You, for the Fool has said in his heart that God does not exist?[25] But surely when this very Fool hears the words "something than which nothing greater[26] can be thought," he understands what he hears. And what he understands is in his understanding,[27] even if he does not understand [judge] it to exist. Indeed, for a thing to be in the understanding is different from understanding [judging] that this thing exists. For when an artist envisions what he is about to paint,[28] he has it in his understanding, but he does not yet understand [judge] that there exists what he has not yet painted. But after he has painted it, he has it in his understanding and he understands [judges] that what he has painted exists. So even the Fool is convinced that something than which nothing greater can be thought exists at least in his understanding; for when he hears of this being, he understands [what he hears], and whatever is understood is in the understanding. But surely that than which a greater cannot be thought cannot be only in the understanding. For if it were only in the understanding, it could be thought to exist also in reality – which is greater [than existing only in the understanding]. Therefore, if that than which a greater cannot be thought existed only in the understanding, then that than which a greater *cannot* be thought would be that than which a greater *can* be thought! But surely this conclusion is impossible. Hence, without doubt, something than which a greater cannot be thought exists both in the understanding and in reality.[29]

Chapter Three: God cannot be thought not to exist.

Assuredly, this being exists so truly [really] that it cannot even be thought not to exist. For there can be thought to exist something whose non-existence is inconceivable; and this thing is greater than anything whose non-existence is conceivable. Therefore, if that than which a greater cannot be thought could be thought not to exist, then that than which a greater cannot be thought would not be that than which a greater cannot be thought – a contradiction. Hence, something than which a greater cannot be thought exists so truly [really] that it cannot even be thought not to exist.

And You are this being, O Lord our God. Therefore, Lord my God, You exist so truly [really] that You cannot even be thought not to exist. And this is rightly the case. For if any mind could conceive of something better than You, the creature would rise above the Creator and would sit in judgment over the

Creator – an utterly preposterous consequence. Indeed, except for You alone, whatever else exists can be conceived not to exist. Therefore, You alone exist most truly [really] of all and thus most greatly of all; for whatever else there is does not exist as truly [really] as You and thus does not exist as much as do You.[30] Since, then, it is so readily clear to a rational mind that You exist most greatly of all, why did the Fool say in his heart that God does not exist?[31] Why indeed except because he is foolish and simple!

Chapter Four: How the Fool said in his heart what cannot be thought.

Yet, since to say something in one's heart is to think it, how did the Fool say in his heart what he was not able to think, or how was he unable to think what he did say in his heart? Now, if he really – rather, since he really – both thought [what he did] because he said it in his heart and did not say it in his heart because he was unable to think it, then there is not merely one sense in which something is said in one's heart, or is thought. For in one sense an object is thought when the word signifying it is thought, and in another when what the object is [i.e., its essence] is understood. Thus, in the first sense but not at all in the second, God can be thought not to exist. Indeed, no one who understands what God is can think that God does not exist, even though he says these words [viz. "God does not exist"] in his heart either meaninglessly or else bizzarely.[32] For God is that than which a greater cannot be thought. Anyone who comprehends (*bene intelligit*) this, surely understands (*intelligit*) that God so exists that He cannot even conceivably not exist. Therefore, anyone who understands that this is the manner in which God exists[33] cannot think that He does not exist.

I thank You, good Lord, I thank You that what at first I believed through Your giving, now by Your enlightening I so understand that even if I did not want to believe that You exist, I could not fail to understand [that You exist].[34]

Chapter Five: God is whatever it is better to be than not to
be. He alone, existing through Himself,
creates all else from nothing.

What, then, are You, Lord God, than whom nothing greater can
be thought? What in fact are You except that which – as highest
of all things, alone existing through Himself – created all else
from nothing? For whatever is not this is less great than can be
conceived. But You cannot be thought to be less great than can
be conceived. Therefore, what good is lacking to the Supreme
Good, through whom every good exists? Consequently, You
are just, truthful, blessed, and whatever it is better to be than
not to be.[35] For it is better to be just than not just, blessed than
not blessed.

Chapter Six: How God is perceptive even though He is not
corporeal.

Now, since to be perceptive, omnipotent, merciful, and impassible is better than not to be [any of these], how are You able to
perceive if You are not corporeal, or how are You omnipotent if
You cannot do all things, or how are You consistently both
merciful and impassible? For if only corporeal things are able
to perceive (inasmuch as the senses belong to a body and are in a
body), how are You able to perceive, since You are not corporeal but are the Supreme Spirit, who is better than what is
corporeal? But if perceiving is only knowing or only for the sake
of knowing (for anyone who perceives knows in accordance with
the characteristic capabilities of the respective senses – e.g.,
colors are known through sight, flavors through taste), then
whatever in some way knows is acceptably said in some way to
perceive. Therefore, Lord, even though You are not corporeal,
truly You are supremely perceptive in the sense of knowing
supremely all things rather than in the sense of knowing by
means of bodily senses, as does an animal.

Chapter Seven: How He is omnipotent although there are
many things which He cannot do.

But how are You omnipotent if You cannot do all things? Or
how can You do all things if You are not able to be corrupted or to
tell a lie or to make what is true be false – for example, to make
what has already happened not to have happened – and the like?[36]
Or is the "ability" to do these things not power but lack of
power?[37] For anyone who is able to do these things is able to do
what is disadvantageous to himself and what he ought not to do.
And the more he is able to do these things, the more powerful
are adversity and perversity over him and the less powerful he is
against them. Therefore, anyone who in this sense is able, is able
not by a power but by a lack of power. For it is not the case that
he is called able because he himself is able; rather [he is called
able] because his own lack of power causes something else to be
powerful over him – or [for some other reason coinciding] with
some other way of speaking. For we say many things improperly –
for example, when we substitute "to be" for "not to be" and
substitute "to do" for "not to do" or for "to do nothing."[38]
Indeed, we often say to someone who denies that something is the
case, "Yes, it's as you say it is," although we would say more
properly, "It's not, as you say it's not."[39] Likewise, we say,
"This man is sitting even as that man is also doing" or 'This
man is resting even as that man is also doing" – although sitting
is not doing anything and resting is doing nothing. Thus, when
someone is said to have the ability to cause or to experience what
is disadvantageous to himself or what he ought not to cause or
experience, this so-called ability is understood to be an inability.
For the more he has the alleged ability, the more powerful are
adversity and perversity over him and the more powerless he is
against them. Therefore, Lord God, You are more truly omnipotent because none of Your abilities are really inabilities and
because nothing has any power over You.

Chapter Eight: How He is merciful and impassible.

But how are You consistently both merciful and impassible?

For if You are impassible You have no compassion. And if You do not have compassion, You do not have a heart sorrowful out of compassion for the wretched – the very thing which being merciful is. And if You are not merciful, from where do the wretched derive their great consolation? How, then, are You both merciful and not merciful, Lord, except because You are merciful for us and not merciful in Yourself? Indeed, You are merciful according to our experience but not merciful according to Your experience. For when You behold us in our pitiable condition, we feel the effect of Your mercy; but You do not feel any emotion. And so You are merciful because You save us miserable creatures and spare us though we sin against You. And You are not merciful, because You experience no compassion for misery.

Chapter Nine: How He who is completely and supremely just spares the wicked. He is justly merciful to the wicked.

But how can You spare the wicked if You are completely and supremely just?[40] For how can He who is completely and supremely just do something which is not just? Or how is it just to give eternal life to one deserving eternal death? How, then, good Lord – good both to those who are good and to those who are wicked – how can You save the wicked if it is not just for them to be saved and if You do only what is just? Inasmuch as Your goodness is incomprehensible, is this reason hidden in the inaccessible light in which You dwell?[41] Truly in the deepest and inmost seat of Your goodness is hidden a fount from which the stream of Your mercy flows. For although You are completely and supremely just, nevertheless because You are completely and supremely good You are also beneficent to the wicked. Indeed, You would be less good if You were beneficent to none of the wicked. For someone who is good both to those who are good and to those who are wicked is better than someone who is good only to those who are good. And someone who is good by virtue of both punishing and sparing the wicked is better than someone who is good by virtue of merely punishing the wicked. Therefore, You are merciful because You are completely and supremely good. Now, although we do perhaps discern why You reward with good things those who are good and with evil things those who are evil, surely we are completely baffled as to why You, who are completely just and in need of no one else, give good things to those who are wicked and guilty in Your sight. O God, the depth of Your goodness! We see why You are merciful, and yet we do not fully see why. We see from where the stream [of Your mercy] flows, and yet we do not see the fount itself from which it flows. Out of Your abundant goodness You are gracious to those who sin against You; in the depth of Your goodness lies hidden the reason for Your graciousness. For although out of goodness You reward with good things those who are good and with evil things those who are evil, the principle of justice seems to require this. But when You give good things to those who are evil, we know that as supremely good You willed to do this, but we wonder why as supremely just You were able to will this.

O mercy, from what rich sweetness and sweet richness You flow forth unto us! O fathomless divine goodness, with what affection sinners ought to love You! For You save those who are just because they are just; but You free those who are wicked even though they are justly condemned. You save the just through the aid of their merits; You free the wicked in spite of their demerits. You save the just by taking account of the good which You have given them; You free the wicked by over-looking the evil which You hate. O immense goodness, which so exceeds all understanding, let there come upon me that mercy which proceeds from Your so great richness! Let there flow into me the mercy which flows out of You! Spare me out of mercy; do not punish me out of justice! For although it is difficult to understand how Your mercy is compatible with Your justice, it is necessary to believe that mercy is not at all opposed to justice, because mercy flows forth from goodness, which does not exist without justice – indeed goodness is truly concordant with justice. If You are merciful because You are supremely good, and if You are supremely good only because You are supremely just, then surely You are merciful because You are supremely just. Help me, just and merciful God, whose light I seek; help me to understand what I am saying. Truly, then, You are merciful because You are just.

Is not Your mercy, then, begotten from Your justice? Do You not, then, spare the wicked out of justice? If so, Lord, if so, then teach me how so. Is it because it is just for You to be so good that You cannot be understood to be any better, and [because it is just for You] to work so powerfully that You cannot be thought to work more powerfully? For what is more just than [Your being so good and so powerful]? But surely You would not be so perfectly just if You were good only by way of retribution and not also by way of mercy, and if You were to make good men only from those who are not good instead of also from those who are evil. And so, in this way, it is just that You spare the wicked and that You make good men from evil ones. In short, that which is not done justly ought not to be done; and what ought not to be done is done unjustly. Therefore, if You were not justly merciful to the wicked, it would be the case that You ought not to be merciful to them; and if You ought not to be merciful, then You would be unjustly merciful. Now, if it is wrong to say that You are unjustly merciful to the wicked, then it is right to believe that You are justly merciful to them.

Chapter Ten: How He justly punishes and justly spares the
the wicked.

Yet, it is also just that You punish the wicked. For what is more just than for those who are good to receive what is good and for those who are evil to receive what is evil? But, then, how is it just for You to punish the wicked and likewise just for You to spare them? Do You justly punish them in one respect and justly spare them in another?

When You punish the wicked, it is just [for You to do so] because punishment corresponds to their merits. But when You spare the wicked, it is just [for You to do so], not because sparing them corresponds to their merits, but because it befits Your goodness. For in sparing the wicked, You are *just* in Yourself but not just from our viewpoint, even as You are merciful from our viewpoint but not merciful in Yourself. For in saving us whom You could justly damn, You are *just* because You do what befits You as supremely good and not because You requite us as we deserve, even as You are merciful because we feel the effect of Your mercy and not because You feel any emotion. So, then, without inconsistency You both punish justly and spare justly.

Chapter Eleven: How all the ways of the Lord are mercy and
truth, and yet the Lord is just in all His ways.

But, O Lord, are You not also, in Yourself, just in punishing the wicked ? To be sure, it is just that You be so just that You cannot be thought to be more just. But You would not be the greatest conceivable justice if You rewarded only those who are good with good things but not those who are evil with evil things. For someone who rewards according to their merits both those who are good and those who are evil is more just than someone who rewards only those who are good. Thus, O just and bene- ficent God, in Yourself You are just both when You punish and when You spare. Truly, then, all the ways of the Lord are mercy and truth, and yet the Lord is just in all His ways.[42] And assuredly these two statements are not incompatible, because it is not just that those whom You will to punish should be saved, nor just that those whom You will to spare should be condemned. For only what You will is just, and only what You do not will is not just. So, then, Your mercy is begotten from Your justice because it is just for You to be good to such an extent that You are good even in sparing. And perhaps this is why the one who is supremely just can will good things for the wicked. But if we can somehow grasp why You can will to save the wicked, surely we cannot at all understand why from among those who are equally wicked You save some and not others because of Your supreme goodness, and condemn some and not others because of Your supreme justice.

Therefore, You are truly perceptive, omnipotent, merciful, and impassible as well as living, wise, good, happy, eternal, and whatever it is better to be than not to be.[43]

Chapter Twelve: God is the life by which He lives, and
similarly for similar attributes.

But surely whatever You are You are through no other than through yourself. Therefore, You are the life by which You live, the wisdom by which You comprehend, and the goodness by which You are good both to those who are good and to those who are evil, and similarly for similar attributes.[44]

Chapter Thirteen: How He alone is unlimited and eternal, although other spirits are also unlimited and eternal.

Now, anything which is at all in space or time is less great than that which is not at all subject to the law of space or time. Therefore, since there is nothing greater than You, no space or time confines You, but You exist everywhere and always. Because this can be said of You alone, You alone are unlimited and eternal. But how, then, are other spirits also said to be unlimited and eternal?

To be sure, You alone are eternal because You alone of all beings do not begin to be, even as You do not cease to be. Yet, how are You alone unlimited? Is a created spirit, although unlimited in comparison with something corporeal, limited in comparison with You? Now, that which while existing somewhere as a whole is not able at the same time to exist elsewhere is certainly limited in every respect – as is seen to be the case with corporeal objects only. And what exists at once everywhere as a whole is unlimited – as is understood to be the case with You alone. But that which while existing somewhere as a whole is able at the same time to exist as a whole elsewhere, but not everywhere, is both limited and unlimited – as is known to be the case with created spirits. For if the soul were not wholly in each of the different parts of the body, the soul as a whole would not experience feeling in each of these parts. Therefore, O Lord, You are uniquely unlimited and eternal; and yet other spirits are also unlimited and eternal.

Chapter Fourteen: How and why God is both seen and not seen by those who seek Him.

My soul, have you found that for which You were looking? You were seeking God, and you have found that He is something highest of all – than which nothing better can be thought. [And you have seen that] this being is life itself, light, wisdom, goodness, eternal blessedness, and blessed eternity, and that this being exists everywhere and always. For if you have not found your God, how is He this being which you have found and which with such certain truth and true certainty you have understood Him to be? On the other hand, if you have found Him, why is it that you do not perceive what you have found? O Lord God, why does my soul not perceive You if it has found You? Has it not found someone whom it has found to be light and truth? For how has it understood [that You are light and truth] except by seeing light and truth? Was it able to understand anything at all about You except through Your light and Your truth?[45] Therefore, if my soul saw light and truth, it saw You. If it did not see You, it did not see light and truth. Or can it be that it saw light and truth but nevertheless did not see You because although it saw You in some way, it did not see You as You are?[46]

Lord my God, my Creator and Renewer, tell my yearning soul what else You are other than what it has seen, so that it may see clearly what it longs [to see]. My soul strains to see more; but beyond what it has already seen it peers only into darkness. Or better, it does not peer into darkness, for there is no darkness in You;[47] rather it becomes aware that it can see no farther because of its own dimness of vision. Why is this, O Lord? Why is this? Is the eye of the soul darkened as a result of its own weakness, or is it dazzled by Your brilliance? Surely, the soul's eye is both darkened from within and dazzled by You from without. Surely, it is darkened because of its own shortness of vision and overwhelmed by Your immensity; truly it is diminished through its own deficiency and overcome by Your fullness. For how great that Light is from which shines every truth which illumines the rational mind! How complete that Truth is in which all truths reside and outside of which there is only what is false and nothing! How immense that Truth is which beholds in one spectrum all created things and beholds by whom, through whom, and in what manner all things were created from nothing! What purity, what simplicity, what assurance and splendor are present there.· Surely these are beyond the comprehension of any creature.

Chapter Fifteen: He is greater than can be thought.

Therefore, O Lord, not only are You that than which a greater cannot be thought, but You are also something greater than can be thought.[48] For since something of this kind can be thought [viz., something which is greater than can be thought], if You were not this being then something greater than You could be thought – a consequence which is impossible.

Chapter Sixteen: This is the inaccessible light in which He dwells.

Truly, O Lord, this is the inaccessible light in which You dwell.[49] For truly nothing else can penetrate this light so that it sees You dwelling there. Truly, then, I cannot stand to look at this light because it is too resplendent for me. Nevertheless, whatever I see I see by means of this light – even as a frail eye sees what it does by means of sunlight, which it could not stand to look at in the sun itself. My understanding is not able to comprehend this light, which shines forth too brilliantly. [My understanding] does not grasp it; and the eye of my soul cannot bear to gaze at length upon it. [My soul's eye] is dazzled by its splendor, overcome by its fullness, overwhelmed by its immensity, confounded by its capacity. O supreme and inaccessible Light, O complete and blessed Truth, how distant You are from me who am so near for You! How far removed You are from my sight though I am so present to Yours! You are wholly present everywhere, and yet I do not behold You. In You I move and exist,[50] and yet I cannot approach You. You are within me and round about me, and yet I do not perceive You.

Chapter Seventeen: Harmony, fragrance, succulence, softness, and beauty are in God in an ineffable manner.

Amidst Your blessedness and light, O Lord, You are still hidden from my soul. Therefore, my soul still dwells in its own wretchedness and darkness. For it looks in all directions but does not see Your beauty. It listens but does not hear Your harmony. It fills its nostrils but does not smell Your fragrance. It tastes but does not savor Your succulence. It feels but does not detect Your softness. Indeed, You possess all of these features ineffably, Lord God – You who gave these features to Your creatures to possess sensibly. But the senses of my soul have been stiffened and made dull and impaired by the oldtime infirmity of sin.

Chapter Eighteen: There are no parts in God or in the eternity which He is.

And, behold, once again confusion,[51] once again sorrow and grief beset me as I seek joy and gladness.[52] My soul hoped for fullness; and, lo, once again it is overwhelmed with need. I desired to eat, and lo, the more I hunger! I tried to mount upward to the divine light and lapsed downward into my own darkness. Indeed, not only did I fall into darkness but I feel enshrouded by it. I fell before my mother conceived me.[53] Surely I was conceived in darkness and born surrounded by it. Surely once long ago we all fell in Adam,[54] in whom we all sinned. In him (who easily possessed but evilly lost for himself and us) we all lost that which we, desiring, do not know how to seek; seeking, do not find; finding, do not find to be what we are seeking. Help me, O Lord, because of Your goodness.[55] I have sought Your countenance; Your countenance, Lord, will I seek. Do not turn Your face from me.[56] Raise me out of myself and unto You. Cleanse, heal, focus, illumine[57] the eye of my mind so that it may behold You.[58] Let my soul muster all its strength and with all its understanding stretch forth once more unto You, O Lord. What are You, what are You, O Lord? What shall my heart understand You to be? Certainly You are life, wisdom, truth, goodness, blessedness, eternity – You are every true good. These are many things; and my limited understanding cannot in a single view behold so many at once in order to delight in all at once. How, then, O Lord, are You all these things? Are they Your parts, or, instead, is each one of them wholly what You are?

Now, whatever is composed of parts is not absolutely one but is in a way many and is different from itself and can be divided either actually or conceivably (*intellectu*). But these consequences are foreign to You, than whom nothing better can be thought. Therefore, there are no parts in You, Lord. Instead of being composite You are something so one and so identical with Yourself that in no respect are You dissimilar to Yourself. Indeed, You are Unity itself, divisible in no respect (*nullo intellectu*). Therefore, life and wisdom and the other characteristics are not parts of You but are all one; and each one of them is wholly what You are and wholly what all the others are. Thus, since neither You nor the eternity which You are has any parts, You and Your eternity are never anywhere as a part; but You exist everywhere as a whole, and Your eternity exists always as a whole.

Chapter Nineteen: He is not in space and time; but all things are in Him.

But if through Your eternity You were, You are, and You will be, and since (1) being past is different from being future and (2) being present is different from being past and from being future, how does Your eternity exist always as a whole? Does none of Your eternity pass by so that it no longer is, and is none of it going to become what, so to speak, it not yet is? Then, in no case *were* You yesterday or *will* You *be* tomorrow; instead, yesterday, today, and tomorrow You *are*. Or better, You simply *are* – existing beyond all time. You do not exist yesterday or today or tomorrow; for yesterday, today, and tomorrow are nothing other than temporal distinctions. Now, although without You nothing can exist, You are not in space or time but all things are in You. For You are not contained by anything but rather You contain all else.[59]

Chapter Twenty: He is before and beyond all things – even all eternal things.

Therefore, You fill and encompass all things; You are before and beyond all things. Now, You are before all things because before they were made You already are.[60] But how are You beyond all things? Indeed, how are You beyond those things which will have no end? Is it because they cannot at all exist without You, whereas You would not at all be less great were they to return to nothing?[61] For in this way You do, after a fashion, surpass them. Is it also because they can be thought to have an end, whereas You cannot at all [be thought to have an end]? For in fact they do in this respect have a kind of end, whereas You do not in any respect [have an end]. Now, surely what in no way has an end surpasses that which in some way has an end. Do You also surpass even all eternal things in that both Your eternity and theirs is present to You as a whole, whereas they do not yet have that part of their eternity which is yet to come, even as they no longer have that part which is already past? Indeed, then, You always surpass them, both because You are always [wholly] present to Yourself and because there is always present to You what is not yet present to them.

Chapter Twenty-one: Whether His eternity has one dimension or many dimensions.

Does Your eternity, then, have one dimension or many dimensions?[62] For as the temporal dimension encompasses all things temporal, so Your eternity encompasses the dimensions of temporality. Indeed, Your eternity has only one dimension with respect to its indivisible unity, but it has many dimensions with respect to its endless immensity. Moreover, although You are so great, O Lord, that all things are filled with Your presence and are in You, nevertheless You are so free from all spatial determination that You have neither center nor halves nor any parts.[63]

Chapter Twenty-two: He alone is what He is and who He is.

Therefore, O Lord, You alone are what You are and who You are. Now, anything whose parts are different from its whole, and in which there is anything mutable, is not absolutely what it is. And what (1) began to exist from not-being, (2) can be thought not to exist, (3) would return to not-being except for the fact that it exists through something else, (4) has a past which it no longer is, and (5) has a future which it not yet is – this does not exist in the unqualified and proper sense of "existing."[64] But You are what You are, because whatever You once in any respect are You are always and wholly.

And in a proper and unqualified sense You are who You are,[65] because You have neither a past nor a future but only a present, and because You cannot be thought ever not to be. And You are life and light and wisdom and blessedness and eternity and many such good things. Nevertheless, You are only one supreme good, altogether sufficient unto Yourself, needing nothing else but needed by all else in order to exist and to fare well.

Chapter Twenty-three: This good is Father, Son, and Holy Spirit equally – and is the one necessary Being, which is every good, complete good, and the only good.

You, God the Father, are this good; and Your Word, i.e., Your Son, is this good.[66] For in the Word in which You speak Yourself there cannot be anything other than what You are or anything greater or lesser than You. For Your Word is as true as You are truthful; and so it is the very Truth that You are – not a different truth from You. You are so simple [in nature] that from You cannot be begotten anything other than what You are.

The one Love common to You and to Your Son, viz., the Holy Spirit who proceeds from You both, is also this same good.[67] Now, this Love is not unequal to You or Your Son; for in proportion to Your greatness You love Yourself and Your Son, and in proportion to His greatness He loves Himself and You. And what is not unequal to You and to Him is not something different from what You and He are. Nor can there proceed from Supreme Simplicity anything which is other than what the one from whom it proceeds is. But that which each one (considered distinctly) is, this the Trinity – Father, Son, and Holy Spirit – is as a whole and all together. For each, distinctly, is nothing other than a supremely simple unity and supremely singular simplicity which cannot be made multiple and cannot be complex.

Now, one thing is necessary,[68] viz., the one necessary Being in which there is every good – or better, who is every good,[69] one good, complete good, and the only good.

Chapter Twenty-four: A conjecture about what kind of good
                                            this is and about how great it is.

And now, my soul, arouse and elevate your whole understanding; ponder as best you can what kind of good this is and how great it is. For if the individual good things are enjoyable, reflect attentively upon how enjoyable is that Good which contains the joyfulness of all good things. This is not the kind of joyfulness experienceable in created things but rather [a kind] as different [from that kind] as the Creator is different from the creature. For if created life is good, how good must be that Life which creates! If earthly security (*salus*) is enjoyable, how enjoyable must be the Salvation (*salus*) which causes all security and salvation! If the wisdom which knows created things is worthy of love, how worthy of love must be the Wisdom which created all things from nothing! In short, if there are many great joys in enjoyable things, how rich and how great must be the joy [to be found] in Him who made these enjoyable things!

Chapter Twenty-five: The kinds and number of goods for
                                            those who enjoy this Good.

O what he shall have who will enjoy this Good, and what he shall not have! Surely, he shall have what he shall want and shall not have what he shall not want.[70] Indeed, he shall there possess the goods of the body and the soul – goods of such kind as the eye has not seen nor the ear heard nor the human heart conceived.[71] O insignificant man, why then do you go from one good to another in quest of what is good for your soul and good for your body? Love the one Good in which are all goods, and it shall suffice you. Desire the simple Good which itself is every good, and it shall be enough for you. For what do you love, O my flesh; what do you desire, O my soul? It is there; all that both of you love is there, all that you desire. Does *beauty* delight you? The just shall shine forth as the sun.[72] Do you take delight in the *swiftness, strength,* or *freedom of* a *body* which nothing can resist? The just shall be like the angels of God[73] because their bodies are sown as fleshly but will rise as spiritual[74] – bodies spiritual, of course, in power not in nature. Do you desire a *long* and *sound life*? A sound eternity and an eternal soundness is there, because the just shall live forever[75] and the salvation of the just comes from the Lord.[76] Do you desire *fullness*? They shall be filled when the glory of God is manifested.[77] Do you desire *intoxication*? They shall be intoxicated with the abundance of the house of God.[78] Do you want *melody*? There choirs of angels sing to God without end. Do you desire any *pleasure* whatsoever that is not impure? God shall grant to them to drink from the torrent of His pleasure.[79] Do you desire *wisdom*? The wisdom of God shall be manifested unto them.[80] Do you delight in *friendship*? They shall love God more than themselves and shall love one another as themselves;[81] and God shall love them more than they love themselves. For through Him they shall love Him and themselves and one another; but He loves Himself and them through Himself. Do you want *unison*? They shall all have one will, because they shall have no will except the will of God. Do you desire *power*? They shall be all-powerful in will, even as God is all-powerful in will. For as God is able to do through Himself that which He wills, so they shall be able to do through Him that which they shall will. For as they shall will nothing other than He shall will, so He shall will whatever they shall will. And what He shall will must come to pass. Do *honor* and *riches* delight you? God shall set His good and faithful servants over many things;[82] indeed, they shall be, as well as be called, sons of God[83] and gods.[84] And where His Son shall be, there they too shall be,[85] for they are heirs of God and joint-heirs with Christ.[86] Do you want true *security*? Surely they shall be certain that they shall never in any way lack these many goods – or rather this one Good – even as they shall be certain (1) that they shall not lose it of their own free wills, (2) that God, who loves them, shall not rend it away from them against their wills while they are loving Him, and (3) that nothing more powerful than God shall separate them from God against their wills.[87]

But where goodness of such quality and of such enormity is present, how rich and how extensive must be the corresponding joy! O human heart, heart beset with need, heart versed in tribulation – yea, overwhelmed with tribulation – how much you would rejoice were you to abound in all these goods! Ask your inmost self whether it can contain its own joy in being so immensely happy. Now surely, if someone else whom you loved in every respect as you do yourself were also to have such happiness, then your own joy would be doubled; for you would rejoice for him no less than for yourself. And if two or three or many more persons were to have such happiness, you would rejoice for each of them as much as for yourself – assuming that you loved each as you do yourself. Therefore, in the case of that perfect love whereby countless happy angels and men shall each love the other no less than himself, each one shall rejoice for every other as much as for himself. So, then, if the heart of man shall scarcely be able to contain its own joy over its own so great good, how shall it be able to contain so many other equally immense joys?

Surely, each person rejoices in another's good fortune to the extent that he loves this other. Therefore, in that perfect happiness, just as each person will love God incomparably more than himself and all those who are with himself, so each will rejoice inestimably more over the happiness of God than over either his own happiness or that of all the others who are with himself. But if with all his heart, all his mind, and all his soul[88] each [of the just] shall so love God that his whole heart, whole mind, and whole soul will not exhaust God's worthiness to be loved, surely with all his heart, all his mind, and all his soul each shall so rejoice that his whole heart, whole mind, and whole soul will not be able to contain the fullness of that joy.

Chapter Twenty-six: Whether this is the full joy which the Lord promises.

My Lord and my God, my hope and my heart's joy, tell my soul whether this is the joy about which You speak to us through Your Son, who said: Ask and you shall receive, so that your joy may be full.[89] For I have found an abundant joy – even a superabundant joy. Indeed, when the heart, the mind, the soul – when the whole man – is filled with that joy, there will still remain joy without limit. Therefore, the whole of Your joy will not enter into those who are rejoicing; instead they will all enter into Your joy. Speak, O Lord, and tell Your servant in his heart whether this is the joy into which Your servants will enter when they will enter into the joy of their Lord.[90] Now, surely no eye has seen, no ear has heard – nor has there entered into the heart of man – that joy in which Your elect ones will rejoice.[91] Therefore, I have not yet thought or said, O Lord, how much Your blessed ones will rejoice. Surely, they will rejoice in the degree that they will love. And they will love in the degree that they will know. How much will they know You in that day, Lord; how much will they love You? Surely, in this life no eye has seen, no ear has heard, nor has there entered into the heart of man how much they will know and love You in the next life.

O God, I pray, let me know and love You, so that I may rejoice in You. And if I cannot in this life [know, love, and rejoice in You] fully, let me advance day by day until the point of fullness comes. Let knowledge of You progress in me here and be made full [in me] there. Let love for You grow in me here and be made full [in me] there, so that here my joy may be great with expectancy while there being full in realization. O Lord, through Your Son You command – or rather, You counsel – us to ask; and through Him You promise that we shall receive, so that our joy may be full.[92] O Lord, I ask for what You counsel through our marvellous Counsellor;[93] may I receive what You promise through Your Truth, so that my joy may be full. God of truth, I ask to receive it, so that my joy may be full. Until then, let my mind meditate upon [what You have promised], let my tongue speak of it. Let my heart love it; let my mouth proclaim it. Let my soul hunger for it; let my flesh thirst for it;[94] let my whole being desire it until such time as I enter into the joy of my Lord,[95] the triune God, blessed forever.[96] Amen.

ON BEHALF OF THE FOOL
by
Gaunilo, monk of Marmoutier

What Someone,[1] on Behalf of the Fool,[2] Replies to
These Arguments

[1][3] To one who doubts whether there exists or denies that there exists a nature than which nothing greater can be thought, the claim is made that the existence of this nature is proven from two considerations: first, from the fact that the very one who doubts or denies the existence of this nature already has this nature in his understanding when, upon hearing it spoken of, he understands what is said; and, secondly, from the fact that, necessarily, what he understands exists not only in his understanding but also in reality. This second consideration is [allegedly] established by the following reasoning:

> To exist also in reality is greater than to exist solely in the understanding. Now, if this thing existed solely in the understanding, then whatever[4] existed also in reality would be greater than it. Thus, that which is greater than all others[5] would be less than some other and would not be greater than all others – surely a contradiction. Therefore, it is necessary that that which is greater than all others (having already been shown to exist in the understanding) exist not only in the understanding but also in reality. For otherwise it could not be that which is greater than all others.

When these claims are made, the doubter or denier [i.e.. the Fool] can perhaps make the replies which follow.

[2][6] Regarding the fact that this thing is said to exist in my understanding simply because I understand what is said, I ask: Could I not similarly be said to have in my understanding – because if someone were to speak of them I would understand whatever he said – all manner of unreal things that in no way actually exist? But suppose that this thing [than which nothing greater can be thought] were proven to be such that it is not able to exist in thought in the same way as any unreal and doubtfully real things do. And, accordingly, suppose that when I have heard of it I am not said to think it (or to have it in thought) but am said to understand it (and to have it in the understanding) since

I could not think it except by understanding (i.e., by apprehending with certainty) that it really exists.⁷ But if this were so, then (to begin with) there would no longer be a difference here between first having this thing in the understanding and subsequently understanding [judging] this thing to exist – as happens in the case of a painting, which first is in the artist's mind and then later is an actual product. Secondly, it could scarcely be plausible that when this thing is spoken of or heard of it could not be thought not to exist in the way even God can [be thought] not to exist. For if this thing cannot [be thought not to exist], why was your entire argument enjoined against one who doubts or denies that there is any such nature as this? Lastly, the claim "This being is such that as soon as it is thought of it must be indubitably understood to exist in reality" would have to be proved to me by an indubitable argument. [It can] not [be proven to me] by the argument that this thing is already in my understanding when I understand what I have heard. For I still maintain that in my understanding there could likewise be whatever other dubiously real and even unreal things are spoken of by someone whose words I have understood. And it would be all the more true [that they are in my understanding] if I, who do not yet believe that this thing [exists], were mistakenly to believe that those things [exist], as often happens.

[3] Hence, the example about the painter's already having in his understanding a picture which he is going to paint would be irrelevant to your argument. For before the painting was made it existed in the painter's art (*arte*). And such a thing in the artist's art is nothing other than a part of the artist's understanding. For as St Augustine says:

> When a craftsman is about to make a chest, he first has it in his art. The chest which is produced is not alive; but the chest which is in the art is alive because the soul of the craftsman is alive, and in it exist all these artefacts before they are produced.⁸

For why are these artefacts alive in the living soul of the craftsman except because they are nothing other than his soul's knowledge and understanding? But except for things which are known to pertain to the very nature of the mind, whenever anything that is heard of or thought of is understood to be real, then without doubt the real thing is different from the understanding by which it is apprehended. Therefore, even if it is true that there exists something than which a greater cannot be thought, nevertheless when it was heard of and understood it would not be like an as yet unproduced painting in the understanding of a painter.[9]

[4] To this may be added a point previously alluded to: viz., that upon hearing of that which is greater than all others that can be thought (which is said to be able to be no other than God Himself), I cannot think of this thing (or have it in the understanding) by reference to any object known to me through species or genus – just as in this way I also cannot think of God Himself (whom surely, for this reason, I can indeed think not to exist). For neither am I acquainted with God Himself nor am I able to infer [what God is like] by reference to some other similar being, since, as even you maintain, God is such that there cannot be anything else similar to Him.[10] Now, suppose that I were to hear something being said about a man totally a stranger to me – a man whom I was not even sure existed. Still, I would be able to think of him by means of the specific or generic notion by which I know what a man is (or what men are) – i.e., by reference to the very thing a man is. However, it could happen that the one who told [me about this stranger] was lying and that the man whom I thought of does not exist. Nonetheless, I would still have conceived of him by reference to the reality which *any* man is, though not by reference to the reality which *that* man is. But when I hear someone speaking of God (or of something greater than all others), I cannot have Him in my thought and understanding in the way that I might have this unreal man in my thought and understanding. For although I can think of a non-existent man by reference to a real thing known to me, I cannot at all think of God except only with respect to the word. And with respect only to a word a real thing can scarcely, if at all, be thought of.[11] For when one thinks with respect to a mere word, he thinks not so much the word itself (i.e., not so much the sound of the letters or syllables), which assuredly is a real thing, as he does the signification of the word that is heard. Yet, [the signification is] not [thought] in the manner of one who knows what is usually meant by the word – i.e., one who thinks in accordance with the thing, whether it is real or exists in thought alone. Rather, [the signification is thought] in the manner of one who does not know what is usually

signified by the word but who (1) thinks only according to the
movement of the mind brought about by hearing this word and
who (2) has difficulty in representing to himself the signification
of what he has heard. (But it would be surprising if he could
ever [in this manner discern] what the thing is.) So, then, it is
still evident that this is the only way something is in my
understanding when I hear and understand someone who
says that there is something greater than all others that can be
thought.

All of this is my reply to the claim that that supreme nature
already exists in my understanding.

[5] Now, I am offered the following proof that, necessarily,
[that supreme nature] exists in reality: Unless it existed in
reality, whatever does exist in reality would be greater than it
and, accordingly, that which was proved assuredly to exist
already in the understanding would not be that which is greater
than all others.

To this argument I reply: If that which cannot even be
properly conceived must nonetheless be said to be in the understanding, then I do not deny that in this improper sense it is in
my understanding. But since from this concession its existence
in reality cannot at all be inferred, I still will not at all concede
that it exists until this existence has been proven to me by an
indubitable argument. Now, whoever says, "This being exists
because otherwise that which is greater than all others would
not be greater than all others" does not pay enough attention to
whom he is speaking. For I do not yet admit – indeed, I even
doubt and deny – that that which is greater [than all others]
exists at all in reality. I do not concede to it any other existence
than that existence (if it should be called existence) present when
the mind tries to represent to itself a thing completely unknown,
[trying to do so] in accordance with a word which it has merely
heard. How, then, from the [alleged] fact that it is, patently, that
which is greater than all others does one prove to me that that
which is greater [than all others] exists in reality? For I still so
doubt and deny it to exist that I claim that this greater [than all
others] is not even in my thought and understanding even in the
way that numerous doubtfully real and uncertainly real things
are. Indeed, I must first be made certain that this greater [than
all others] exists somewhere in reality; only then will I find

indubitable the claim that it exists (also) in reality *because* it is greater than all others.[12]

[6] For example, people tell of an island existing somewhere in the ocean. Some call it Lost Island because of the difficulty – or rather, the impossibility – of finding what is only imaginary.[13] They say that it abounds with inestimable plentitude of riches and delights of all sorts – even much more so than is reported of the Isles of the Blessed. Having no owner or inhabitant [it is said] to excel completely – because of the superabundant goods for the taking – all other lands in which men dwell. Now, should someone tell me these tales I would easily understand what he said, for it is simple enough to comprehend. But suppose he were then to add, as if it followed logically: "You can no more doubt that this island which is more excellent than all other lands exists somewhere in reality than you can doubt that it is in your understanding. And since for it to exist in reality as well as in the understanding is more excellent [than for it to exist in the understanding alone], then, necessarily, it really exists. For if it did not exist, then any other really existing country would be more excellent than it, and thus this island, which has already been understood by you to be more excellent [than all other lands], would not be more excellent [than all others]."[14] Now, if someone wanted in this way to prove to me that I must not any longer doubt the existence of this island, then either I would think he were jesting or else I would not know whom I ought to regard as the more foolish – either myself, were I to grant his argument, or him, were he to suppose that he had proved to any extent the existence of this island. For he would first have to prove that this island's excellence is in my understanding only in the way that a thing which really and certainly exists is in my understanding and not at all in the way that a thing which is unreal or doubtfully real is in my understanding.

[7] So might the Fool answer preliminarily the arguments against his position. And when [his opponent] goes on to maintain that that which is greater [than all others] is such that it cannot even be thought not to exist (this step in turn being proved from no other consideration than that otherwise this being would not be greater than all others), the Fool can point to his previous reply and ask: "When indeed did I ever concede the real existence of such a being (viz., one which is greater

than all others), so that from this concession I could be shown that it exists so greatly in reality that it cannot be thought not to exist? Therefore, first of all one must prove by an indubitable argument that there exists a nature which is higher (i.e., greater or better) than all existing things, so that on the basis of this proof we can go on to deduce all the other characteristics which that which is greater and better than all others must not fail to have."

Now, as for saying that this Supreme Being cannot be *thought* not to exist:[15] one might more appropriately say that it cannot be *understood* not to exist and cannot be understood even to be able not to exist. For properly speaking, unrealities cannot be understood; but they can surely be thought – in the way that the Fool thought that God does not exist.[16] Now, I know most certainly that I exist; yet I know no less certainly that I am able not to exist. Moreover, I understand indubitably that that being which is supreme, viz., God, exists and cannot fail to exist. Still, I do not know whether, during the time when I know most certainly that I exist, I can think that I do not exist. But if I can, why [can I] not [think not to exist] whatever else I know as certainly [as I know my own existence]? On the other hand, if I cannot [think that I do not exist], then this [property of not being able to be thought not to exist] will no longer be uniquely God's.

[8] The other parts of that treatise are argued so truthfully, brilliantly, impressively, and are, in fact, so fully useful and so fully fragrant with an inward perfume of devout and holy affection that they should not at all be despised simply because of those things at the beginning. (To be sure, those matters are rightly discerned, but they are argued less firmly [than the later parts].) Instead, the initial parts must be more cogently argued, so that all parts may be received with great respect and praise.

REPLY TO GAUNILO
by
Anselm

What the Author of That Treatise
Replies to These Objections

Since my arguments are not attacked by the Fool, against whom I directed my treatise, but by an intelligent and orthodox Christian (*catholicus*) on behalf of the Fool, it will suffice to reply to the orthodox Christian (*catholicus*).

[1][1] Now, you argue (whoever you are[2] who claims that the Fool can make these objections) as follows:

Something than which a greater cannot be thought is in the understanding only as something which cannot even be properly conceived. Moreover, from the fact that it (viz., what I am calling *that than which a greater cannot be thought*) exists in the understanding there does not follow that it exists also in reality – any more than there follows that Lost Island most certainly exists, from the fact that when it is described in words the one who hears of it does not doubt that it exists in his understanding.

But I contend that if that than which a greater cannot be thought is not understood or thought and is not in the understanding or in thought, then surely either (1) God is not that than which a greater cannot be thought or else (2) He is not understood or thought and is not in the understanding or in thought. But I point to your faith and conscience as the strongest indicator of how false these inferences are.[3] Therefore, that than which a greater cannot be thought is indeed understood and thought, and is in your understanding and in your thought. Hence, either those premises are not true by which you try to prove the opposite, or else from them there does not follow what you suppose you infer logically.

From the fact that something than which a greater cannot be thought is understood there does not follow, you claim, that it is in the understanding. Or if it is in the understanding, there does not follow, you claim, that it exists in reality. But with confidence I assert that if it can be even thought to exist, it is necessary that it exist. For that than which a greater cannot be thought can only be thought to exist without a beginning. Now, whatever can be thought to exist but does not exist can be thought to begin to exist. Thus, it is not the case that that than which a greater cannot be thought can be thought to exist and yet does not exist. Therefore, if it can be thought to exist, it is necessary that it exist.

Furthermore: if indeed it can be even thought, it is necessary that it exist. For even one who doubts or denies the existence of something than which a greater cannot be thought admits that if this being were to exist it would neither actually nor conceivably (*nec actu nec intellectu*) be able not to exist. For otherwise [i.e., if it existed but were able not to exist] it would not be that than which a greater cannot be thought. Now, as for whatever can be thought but does not exist: if it were to exist, it would either actually or conceivably (*vel actu vel intellectu*) be able not to exist. Therefore, if that than which a greater cannot be thought can be even thought, it is not able not to exist.

But let us suppose that it can be thought and yet does not exist.[4] Now, whatever can be thought and yet does not exist would not, if it were to exist, be that than which a greater cannot be thought. Hence, if that than which a greater cannot be thought [assumed for the sake of the argument not to exist] were to exist, it would not be that than which a greater cannot be thought – an utterly absurd consequence. Therefore, it is false [to suppose] that something than which a greater cannot be thought can be thought and yet does not exist.[5] Consequently, it is all the more [false to suppose] that it can be understood and can be in the understanding [and yet does not exist].

I will add a further point. Consider anything whatsoever which does not exist at some given place or at some given time. Without doubt, even if it does exist elsewhere or at another time, it can be thought never and nowhere to exist – just as it does not exist at that given place or at that given time. For with regard to something which did not exist yesterday but does exist today: just as it is understood not to have existed yesterday, so it can be supposed never to exist. And with regard to something which is not in this place but is in that place: just as it is not in this place, so it can be thought nowhere to exist. Likewise, if some of a thing's parts do not exist where or when its other parts exist, then all of its parts – and thus the thing as a whole – can be thought never and nowhere to exist. For even were we to say that time exists always and that the world exists everywhere, nevertheless it is not the case that time exists always as a whole, or that the world exists everywhere as a whole. Now, just as some parts of time do not exist when others do, so the parts of time can be thought never to exist. And just as some parts of the world do not exist where other parts do, so the parts of the world can be supposed nowhere to exist. Now, even that which is a unified composite is able to be divided in thought and is able not to exist. Therefore, with regard to whatever at some place or time does not exist as a whole: even if this thing does exist, it can be thought not to exist. But with regard to that than which a greater cannot be thought: if it exists, it cannot be thought not to exist. For otherwise,[6] if it existed it would not be that than which a greater cannot be thought – an inconsistency. Therefore, it does not at all fail to exist as a whole at any time or place but exists as a whole always and everywhere.[7]

Don't you think that that thing about which these statements are understood can to some extent be thought and understood, and to some extent can be in thought and in the understanding? For if it cannot [be thought or understood], then the above statements cannot be understood about it. But if you say that what is not fully understood is *not* understood and is not in the understanding, then say as well that someone who cannot stand to gaze upon the most brilliant light of the sun does not see daylight, which is nothing other than the sun's light.[8] Surely that than which a greater cannot be thought is understood and is in the understanding to the extent that the above statements are understood about it.

[II] And so in the argument with which you find fault I said that when the Fool hears of that than which a greater cannot be thought, he understands what he hears. Surely, if it is spoken of in a language one knows, then one who does not understand [what he hears] has little or no intelligence [*intellectus*]. Next, I said that if it is understood, it is in the understanding. (Or would what [I claim] conclusively to have proved to exist in reality not at all[9] exist in the understanding?) Now, you will say that even if it is in the understanding, there does not follow therefrom that it is understood. Notice, [though], that from the fact

of its being understood, there does follow that it is in the understanding. For just as what is thought is thought by thinking,
and what is thought by thinking is thereby in our thinking, so
what is understood is understood by the understanding, and what
is understood by the understanding is thereby in the understanding. What is more obvious than this?

Next, I went on to maintain that if [that than which a
greater cannot be thought] existed only in the understanding, it
could be thought to exist also in reality – which is greater [than
existing only in the understanding]. Therefore, if it existed only
in the understanding, then that than which a greater cannot be
thought would be that than which a greater *can* be thought.
What, I ask, follows more logically? For if it existed only in the
understanding, could it not be thought to exist also in reality?
And if so, would not anyone who thought this [i.e., thought it to
exist in reality] think something greater than it – if it existed
only in the understanding? Therefore, what follows more
logically than this conclusion, viz.: if that than which a greater
cannot be thought existed only in the understanding, it would be
that than which a greater *can* be thought? But surely that than
which a greater cannot be thought is in no sense[10] that than
which a greater can be thought. Does it not follow, therefore,
that if that than which a greater cannot be thought is at all[11] in
the understanding, then it does not exist in the understanding
alone? For if it existed only in the understanding it would be
that than which a greater *can* be thought – a contradiction.

[III] But you contend that my reasoning proceeds analogously to someone's claiming that an island in the ocean (an
island which because of its abundance excels all other lands and
which because of the difficulty – or rather the impossibility – of
finding what is only imaginary[12] is called Lost Island) cannot be
doubted really to exist since one readily understands when it is
described in words. With confidence I reply: if besides that than
which a greater cannot be thought anyone finds for me anything
else (whether existing in reality or only in thought) to which
he can apply the logic of my argument, then I will find and will
make him a present of that lost island – no longer to be lost.

However, it now seems clear that that than which a greater
cannot be thought is not able to be thought not to exist since it

exists so assuredly and truly. For otherwise [i.e., if it could be *thought* not to exist], it would not at all exist.[13] In fact, if some-one says that he thinks that this thing does not exist, I reply that in thinking as he says, either he is or he is not thinking of some-thing than which a greater cannot be thought. If he is not think-ing of it, then he is not thinking that what he is not thinking of does not exist. And if he is thinking of it, then surely he is think-ing of something which cannot even be thought not to exist. For if it could be thought not to exist, it could be thought to have a beginning and an end. But such a consequence is impossible. Therefore, whoever thinks of this thing thinks of something which cannot even be thought not to exist. Now, whoever thinks of [what cannot be thought not to exist] does not think that it does not exist. Otherwise he would be thinking what can-not be thought. Therefore, it is not the case that that than which a greater cannot be thought can be thought not to exist.

[IV] You suggest that to say "The Supreme Being *cannot be understood* not to exist and cannot be understood even to be able not to exist" might be better than to say "The Supreme Being *cannot be thought* not to exist." [I answer]: It was necessary to say "cannot be thought." For had I said that this thing "cannot be understood not to exist," then perhaps you – who say that, strictly speaking, unrealities cannot be understood – might have objected that nothing which exists can be under-stood not to exist. For it is false that what exists does not exist; and, thus, it would not be a unique characteristic of God not to be able to be understood not to exist. On the other hand, if any one of the things which most assuredly exist *can* be understood not to exist, then likewise other certainly existing things [e.g., God] can also be understood not to exist. But these objections do not hold with regard to *thinking* – as careful reflection will show. For even if no existing things could be *understood* not to exist, still they could all be *thought* not to exist – with the exception of that which exists supremely. Indeed, all and only things which have a beginning or an end or are composed of parts – and whatever (as I have already said) at any place or time does not exist as a whole – can be thought not to exist. But only that in which there is no conceivable beginning or end or combination of parts, and only that which exists as a whole everywhere and always, cannot be thought not to exist.

Be aware, then, that you can think that you do not exist even while knowing most certainly that you do exist. (I am surprised that you expressed uncertainty about this point.) For many things which we know to exist we think not to exist; and many things which we know not to exist we think to exist. [In so thinking] we do not judge – rather we imagine – that [these things] are as we think. Indeed, [both of the following statements are true:] (1) We can think that something does not exist even while knowing that it does exist; for we can think [imagine] the one state while at the same time knowing the other. And (2) we cannot think that something does not exist while knowing that it does exist; for we cannot think it to exist and at the same time think it not to exist. Hence, if someone distinguishes in this manner these two senses of this expression ["to think"], he will discern (*intelliget*) that (2') a thing cannot be thought not to exist while known to exist and also that (1') anything (except that than which a greater cannot be thought) can be thought not to exist while known to exist. So, then, [in one sense] it is a unique characteristic of God not to be able to be thought not to exist; and [in another sense] many other things, while existing, are also not able to be thought not to exist.[14] But about the way in which God is said to be thought not to exist, I deem that enough has been stated in the treatise itself [i.e., in the *Proslogion*].[15]

[V] It is easy for someone even of moderate intelligence to detect [what is wrong with] the other types of objections which you raise against me on behalf of the Fool; and so I thought I ought to forego showing their misconception. But because I hear that they do seem to various readers to count somewhat against my position, I will examine them briefly.

For one thing, you say repeatedly that I argue as follows: "That which is greater than all others is in the understanding. And if it is in the understanding, it exists also in reality; for otherwise [i.e., if it did not exist in reality], that which is greater than all others would not be that which is greater than all others." But nowhere in any of my statements can such a line of reasoning be found. For the expression "that which is greater than all others" and the expression "that than which a greater cannot be thought" are not equally effective in proving that what is spoken of exists in reality. For if someone claims that that than which a greater cannot be thought (1) is not something really existent or (2) is able not to exist or (3) is able to be thought not to exist, he can easily be refuted. For what does not exist is able not to exist; and what is able not to exist is able to be thought not to exist. But regarding whatever *can* be thought not to exist: if it does exist, it is not that than which a greater cannot be thought. And if it does not exist, then (assuredly) if it were to exist, it would not be that than which a greater cannot be thought. But regarding that than which a greater *cannot* be thought: we cannot say that if it exists it is not that than which a greater cannot be thought, or that if it were to exist it would not be that than which a greater cannot be thought. Therefore, it is evident that [that than which a greater cannot be thought] neither (1) fails to exist nor (2) is able not to exist nor (3) is able to be thought not to exist. For otherwise [i.e., were it able not to exist or able to be thought not to exist], if it exists it is not what it is described as being; and if it were to exist it would not be [what it is described as being].

But this consequence seems more difficult to be able to be deduced in the case of what is said to be greater than all others. For it is not obvious that what can be thought not to exist is not greater than all other existing things, as it is obvious that it is not that than which a greater cannot be thought. And it is not certain that if there is something greater than all others it is identical with that than which a greater cannot be thought (or that if it were to exist it would likewise be identical with [that than which a greater cannot be thought]), as this inference is certain about what is called that than which a greater cannot be thought. For what if someone should say that there exists something which is greater than all other existing things and yet that this thing can be thought not to exist and that something else – even if it does not exist – can be thought to be greater than this thing? Could the inference "Therefore, it is not greater than all other existing things" obviously be drawn in that case – just as the inference "Therefore, it is not that than which a greater cannot be thought" can very obviously be drawn in my argument? The first inference does not follow immediately from appeal to the notion of what is greater than all others; but the second does follow immediately from appeal to the notion of that than which a greater cannot be thought.[16] Therefore, if the argument which speaks of what is greater than all others proceeds less directly than the argument which speaks of that than which a greater cannot be thought, you unjustly criticize me for having said something I did not say; for [what I was interpreted as saying] differs so greatly from what I did say.[17]

On the other hand, if with an additional premise it can [be proven that what is greater than all others exists], you ought not to have criticized me for having said something which can be proven. Now, the possibility of this proof is easily apprehended by one who recognizes that that than which a greater cannot be thought is able to be this [i.e., to be greater than all others]. For that than which a greater cannot be thought can only be understood to be that which alone is greater than all others. Therefore, just as that than which a greater cannot be thought is understood and is in the understanding and hence is affirmed to exist in reality, so what is said to be greater than all others is inferred to be understood and to be in the understanding and hence, necessarily, to exist in reality. Do you see, then, the respect in which you did rightly compare me with that fool who wanted to assert the existence of Lost Island from the mere fact that its description was understood?[18]

[VI] Now, you also object that all kinds of unreal and doubtfully real things can likewise be understood and can be in the understanding in the same way as the thing I was speaking of. Now, I am surprised that here you have argued against me. For I aimed at proving something [which I assumed to be] doubtfully real. And I was content at the outset to show in any manner whatsoever that this thing is understood and is in the understanding, so that thereafter I might go on to determine whether it exists only in the understanding, as unreal things do, or whether it also actually exists, as real things do. For if unreal and uncertainly real things are understood and are in the understanding in the sense that when they are spoken of the hearer understands what the speaker means, then nothing prevents what I have spoken of from being understood and being in the understanding.

But how are the following statements consistent? [On the one hand] you say that if someone spoke of unreal things you would understand whatever he said. And [on the other hand] with regard to that which is present in thought but not in the manner in which unreal things are, you say not that you think it or have it in thought (when you hear of it) but rather that you understand it and have it in the understanding. For [you say that] you can think this [real] thing only by understanding it – i.e., only by apprehending with certainty that it really exists.[19] How, I ask, are these two statements compatible – viz., (1) that unreal objects can be understood and (2) that to understand is to apprehend with certainty that a thing exists? [This contradiction] is not my concern; you attend to it.[20] Yet, if unreal things *are* in some sense understood, and if your definition is a definition of a special mode of understanding rather than of every mode of understanding, then I ought not to have been criticized for having said that that than which a greater cannot be thought is understood and is in the understanding, and [for having said this] even before it was certain that this being exists in reality.

[VII] Next, one can scarcely at all believe, you say, that when this thing is spoken of or heard of, it cannot be thought not to exist, as even God [you say] can be thought not to exist. Yet, let those who have even a minimal knowledge of debate and argumentation come to my defense. For is it reasonable for someone to deny what he understands [and to do so] because it is said to be identical with that which he denies because he does not understand? Or if he ever denies something which to some extent he understands, and if that thing is identical with something which he does not at all understand, is not what is in question more easily proved about that which to some extent he understands than about that which he does not at all[21] understand? Therefore, [on the one hand] it cannot even be plausible for someone to deny any knowledge of that than which a greater cannot be thought (which, when he hears of, he understands to some extent) because he denies any knowledge of God (in no respect thinking the meaning of the word "God"). On the other hand, if he denies any knowledge of God because he does not at all[22] understand [the meaning of the word "God"], then is it not easier to prove what in some sense is understood than what is not at all understood? Therefore, in order to prove that God exists I, not unreasonably, adduced against the Fool [the description] "that than which a greater cannot be thought." For he might not at all understand the word "God," but he would to some extent understand the description.

[VIII] Now, you go to so much trouble to prove that that than which a greater cannot be thought is not in the understanding analogously to the way in which an unproduced painting is in the understanding of an artist. Yet, there was no reason for you to do so. For I introduced the [example of a] preenvisioned painting not because I wanted to assert that the thing I was discussing is analogous to a painting but only so that I could show that something can be in the understanding without being understood [judged] to exist.[23]

Moreover, you maintain that upon hearing of that than which a greater cannot be thought you cannot think it (or have it in the understanding) by reference to any object known to you through species or genus. For [you claim that] you are neither acquainted with this being nor able to conceive of it by reference to some other similar being. Yet, the facts of the matter are clearly otherwise. For to the extent that everything less good is good, to that extent it is like a greater good. Therefore, to any rational mind it is clear that by ascending from lesser goods to higher goods, we can indeed pass from conceiving of those goods than which a greater can be thought to conceiving of that Good than which nothing greater can be thought. Is there anyone, for example – even if he does not believe in the real existence of what he conceives – who is unable to think that if there is something good which has a beginning and an end, then that good is much better which has no end though having a beginning. And just as this second good [which has a beginning but no end] is better than the first, so also that good which has neither a beginning nor an end is better than this second good. [This third good is better than the second] even if the third is always moving from the past through the present toward the future. Yet, that good which in no way needs or is compelled to be changed or moved is far better (whether or not it really exists) than this [third good, which does change]. Can this [unchanging good] not be conceived? Can anything greater than it be conceived? Is not this [i.e., conceiving of this unchanging good] the same as passing from those goods than which a greater can be thought to the conception of that Good than which a greater cannot be thought? Therefore, there is a way to conceive of that than which a greater cannot be thought. Thus, the Fool, who does not accept sacred authority [i.e., Scripture], can easily be refuted if he says that by reference to other things he cannot conceive of that than which a greater cannot be thought. But if an orthodox Christian (*catholicus*) should say this, let him remember that since the creation of the world the invisible things of God (including His eternal power and deity) are clearly seen and are understood by reference to created things.[24]

[IX] Yet, even if it were true that [in one sense] that than which a greater cannot be thought could not be conceived or understood, nonetheless it would not be false that [in another sense] that than which a greater cannot be thought can be conceived and understood. Nothing prevents our saying [the word] "unsayable," even though what is called unsayable cannot be said. Moreover, we can think [the concept] *inconceivable*, even though what is rightly called inconceivable cannot be conceived. By the same token, when that than which nothing greater can be thought is spoken of, without doubt what is heard can be thought and understood, even if the thing than which a greater cannot be thought could not be thought or understood. For even if anyone were so foolish as to say that something than which a greater cannot be thought does not exist, nevertheless he would not be so shameless as to say that he cannot think or understand what he is saying. Or if such an impudent person is found, not only is his word to be rejected but he himself is to be despised. Therefore, whoever denies the existence of that than which a greater cannot be thought surely thinks and understands the denial he is making. And he cannot think or understand this denial without thinking or understanding its parts – one of which is "that than which a greater cannot be thought." Therefore, whoever denies this [viz., that this being exists] thinks and understands [the meaning of] "that than which a greater cannot be thought."

In like manner, obviously, "what is not able not to exist" can be thought and understood. Now, someone who thinks of this [viz., of what is not able not to exist] thinks of something greater than someone who thinks of what is able not to exist. Therefore, while that than which a greater cannot be thought is conceived: if what is able not to exist is conceived, then that than which a greater cannot be thought is not conceived. Now, since the same thing cannot at the same time be both conceived and not conceived, someone who conceives of that than which a greater cannot be thought does not conceive of what is able not to exist but rather conceives of what is not able not to exist. Hence, it is necessarily the case that what he conceives of exists – because whatever is able not to exist is not what he conceives of.

[X] I have now showed, I believe, that in my earlier treatise I proved – not by inconclusive reasoning but by very compelling reasoning – that something than which a greater cannot be thought exists in reality. And [I have showed] that this reasoning was not weakened by any strong counter-reasoning. For the significance of this utterance ["that than which a greater cannot be thought"] contains so much force that what is spoken of is, by the very fact that it is understood or thought, necessarily proved really to exist and to be whatever ought to be believed about the Divine Substance. For we believe about the Divine Substance whatever can in every respect be thought to be better than its contradictory.[25] For example, it is better to be eternal than not to be eternal, better to be good than not to be good – or rather, to be goodness itself than not to be goodness itself. But that than which something greater cannot be thought cannot fail to be anything of this kind. Therefore, it is necessarily the case that that than which a greater cannot be thought is whatever ought to be believed about the Divine Being.

I thank you for your kindness both in criticizing and in praising my treatise. For since you praised so lavishly those things which seemed to you worthy of acceptance, it is quite evident that you criticized out of good will rather than out of malevolence the things which seemed to you untenable.

A MEDITATION ON
HUMAN REDEMPTION

A Meditation on Human Redemption

O Christian soul,[1] soul raised up from grievous death, soul redeemed and freed by the blood of God from wretched bondage: arouse your mind, remember your resurrection, contemplate your redemption and liberation. Consider anew where and what the strength of your salvation is,[2] spend time in meditating upon this strength, delight in reflecting upon it. Shake off your disinclination, constrain yourself, strive with your mind toward this end. Taste the goodness of your Redeemer, be aflame with love for your Savior, chew His words as a honey-comb, suck out their flavor, which is sweeter than honey,[3] swallow their health-giving sweetness. Chew by thinking, suck by understanding, swallow by loving and rejoicing. Rejoice in chewing, be glad in sucking, delight in swallowing.

Where, then, and what is the strength and might of your salvation? Assuredly, Christ has resurrected you. That Good Samaritan has healed you, that Good Friend has redeemed and freed you by [sacrificing] His own soul [life]. Yes, it was Christ. Therefore, the strength of Christ is the strength of your salvation. Where is the strength of Christ? Surely horns are in His hands; there His strength is hidden.[4] Strength is indeed in His hands because His hands were nailed to the arms of the cross. But what strength can there be in such weakness,[5] what majesty in such humiliation, what worthy of reverence in such contempt? But surely because it is [disguised] in weakness it is something hidden, because [veiled] in humiliation it is something concealed, because [covered with] contempt it is something inaccessible. O hidden might! A man appended to a cross suspends the eternal death impending over the human race; a man fastened to a cross unfastens a world affixed to endless death! O concealed power! A man condemned with thieves saves men condemned with demons; a man stretched out on a cross draws all things unto Himself![6] O unseen strength! One soul yielded up in the torment [of crucifixion] draws countless souls from the torments of Hell; a man undergoes bodily death and abolishes spiritual death!

137

Why did you, O good Lord, gracious Redeemer, mighty
Savior, why did You veil such strength with such lowliness?
Was it in order to deceive the Devil, who by deceiving man
thrust him forth from Paradise? Surely, Truth deceives no one;
someone deceives himself if he does not know the truth, if he
does not believe it. He deceives himself if, seeing the truth, he
hates it or despises it; thus, Truth deceives no one. Well, then,
[did You conceal Your power] in order that the Devil might
deceive himself? Surely, just as Truth deceives no one, so it
does not intend that anyone deceive himself, (even though we
do say that Truth intends this when Truth permits it to occur).
For You did not assume a human nature in order to conceal what
was known about You but in order to reveal what was unknown
about You. You said that You were truly divine and truly
human, and You demonstrated this fact through Your works.
The hiddenness was unavoidable, not deliberate. The reason
that the event occurred as it did was not in order to be hidden,
but in order to be performed in the right way. [It happened in
that way] not in order to deceive anyone, but in order to be done
as was fitting. If this event is called concealed, then it is called
so only because it is not revealed to everyone. Although Truth
does not manifest itself to everyone, it does not withhold itself
from anyone. Therefore, O Lord, in becoming incarnate it was
not Your purpose to deceive anyone or to cause anyone to
deceive himself. You remained in the truth in every respect so
that You might do what had to be done in the way it had to be
done. Hence, let anyone who has deceived himself regarding
Your truth complain not about You but about the falsehood in
himself.

Did the Devil justly have against God or against man some
claim which obliged God to act against him on man's behalf in
this manner [i.e., by incarnation] rather than by open force, so
that when the Devil unjustly killed a just man [Jesus] he would
justly lose the power he was holding over unjust men?[7] No,
for surely God did not owe the Devil anything except punishment. Nor did man [owe the Devil anything] except requital,
so that just as man by sinning permitted himself easily to be
defeated by the Devil, so by keeping justice[8] intact even on pain
of death, he would defeat the Devil. But even this [conquering
of the Devil] man owed only to God; for he sinned against God,

not against the Devil. Nor did he belong to the Devil; rather both man and the Devil belonged to God. But even in vexing man the Devil acted not out of zeal for justice but out of zeal for iniquity. God did not command [this vexation]; He only permitted it. God's justice, not the Devil's, required [man's punishment]. Therefore, the Devil had no claim which obliged God to conceal His power or to postpone its use in order to secure man's salvation.

Did some necessity compel the Most High thus to humble Himself as He did; was the Almighty compelled to toil as He did in order to accomplish what He did? No, for all necessity and impossibility are subject to His will. Indeed, what He wills must occur; and what He does not will cannot occur. Therefore, He acted of His own will; and because His will is always good, He acted out of goodness alone. God did not need to secure man's salvation in the way He did; but human nature needed in that way to make satisfaction to God. God did not need to suffer such agony; but man needed to be reconciled through God's sufferings. God did not need to humble Himself through incarnation; but man needed to be rescued from the depth of Hell through God's incarnation. The Divine Nature did not need, and was not able, to be abased or to toil.[9] It was necessary for human nature to do all these things [viz., to make satisfaction, to be reconciled, and to be rescued] in order to be restored to that end for which it was created. But neither human nature nor anyone other than God Himself was able to accomplish these things. Man cannot be restored to that end for which he was made unless he attains to the likeness of those angels in whom there is no sin.[10] This state can only be attained if remission is received for all sins. And this remission is possible only if complete satisfaction has been made.

This satisfaction ought to be such that the sinner or someone on his behalf gives to God something of his own which is not owed – something which exceeds everything that is not God.[11] For to sin is to dishonor God; and man ought not to dishonor God even if [as a consequence] it were necessary for everything that is other than God to be destroyed. Therefore, without doubt, unchanging truth and clear reason demand that the sinner give to God, in place of the honor stolen, something greater than that for which he ought to have refused to dishonor

God.[12] But human nature by itself did not have this payment. And without the required satisfaction human nature could not be reconciled, lest Divine Justice leave a sin unreckoned-with in His kingdom. Therefore, Divine Goodness gave assistance. The Son of God assumed a human nature into His own person, so that in this person He was the God-man, who possessed what exceeded not only every being which is not God but also every debt which sinners ought to pay. And since He owed nothing for Himself, He paid this sum for others who did not have what they were indebted to pay.[13]

For the life of that man [Jesus] is more precious than everything that is not God, and it surpasses every debt owed by sinners as satisfaction. For if putting Him to death [is a sin which] surpasses the multitude and magnitude of all conceivable sins which are not against the person of God, clearly His life is a good greater than the evil of all those sins which are not against the person of God.[14] To honor the Father, that man [Jesus] – who was not obliged to die, because not a sinner – freely gave something of His own when He permitted His life to be taken from Him for the sake of justice. [He permitted this] in order to show to all others by example that they ought not to forsake the justice of God even because of death, which inevitably they are obliged to undergo at some time or other; for He who was not obliged [to undergo] death and who, having kept justice, could have avoided death, freely and for the sake of justice endured death, which was inflicted upon Him. Thus, in that man human nature freely and out of no obligation gave to God something its own, so that it might redeem itself in others in whom it did not have what it, as a result of indebtedness, was required to pay.[15]

In all these occurrences the divine nature [in the God-man] was not abased but the human nature was exalted. The divine nature was not weakened but the human nature was mercifully assisted. Moreover, in that man the human nature did not suffer anything out of necessity but suffered only voluntarily. That man did not succumb to any compelling force; but out of voluntary goodness, and for the honor of God and the benefit of other men, He bore mercifully and laudably what was inflicted upon Him out of malevolence. The requirement of obedience did not constrain Him, but His mighty wisdom disposed Him. For the

Father by His command did not compel that man to die, but that man freely performed what He knew would please the Father and would be helpful to other men. The Father could not compel Him with respect to that which He ought not to have required of Him. The very great honor which the Son with such a good will freely offered to the Father could not fail to please the Father. Thus, when the Son freely willed to do what he knew would please the Father, He displayed free obedience to the Father. Indeed, since the Father gave the Son this good will – a will nonetheless free [i.e., even though bestowed by another] – the Son is rightly said to have received this will as the Father's command.[16] Therefore, in this way, the Son was obedient to the Father even unto death;[17] and He did as the Father commanded;[18] and He drank of the chalice which the Father gave Him.[19] For human nature gave this perfect and completely free obedience when [in Jesus] it freely submitted its own free will to the will of God and when it freely and without any constraint exercised the good will which it had received.

Thus, that man redeemed all other men when what He freely gave to God God reckoned for the debt they owed. Through this payment a man is redeemed from his faults not once only; rather, he is received as often as he returns again in worthy penitence. Nevertheless, this penitence is not promised to the sinner. But since payment was made on the cross, our Christ has redeemed us through the cross. Therefore, those who will to come to this grace with worthy affection are saved; but those who despise this grace are justly condemned because they do not pay the debt they owe.

Behold, O Christian soul, this is the strength of your salvation, this is what has made possible your freedom, this is the cost of your redemption. You were in bondage, but through the cross you have been redeemed. You were a servant, but through the cross you have been set free. You are an exile who in this manner has been led back home, someone lost who has been found, someone dead who has been revived. O man, let your heart feed upon these thoughts, let it chew continually upon them, let it suck upon them and swallow them whenever your mouth receives the body and blood of your Redeemer. In this life make these thoughts your daily bread, your nourishment, your provision. For through these thoughts and only through them will you remain in Christ and Christ in you; and only through them will your joy be full in the life to come.

But You, O Lord, You who underwent death so that I might live, how can I rejoice over my freedom, which results only from Your bonds? How can I be glad about my salvation when it comes only because of Your sorrows? How can I delight in my life, which is secured only by Your death? Shall I rejoice over what You have suffered and over the cruelty of those who have inflicted these sufferings upon You? For had they not done so, You would not have suffered; and had You not suffered, I would not have possessed these goods. On the other hand, if I grieve over Your sufferings, how can I delight in these goods for the sake of which Your sufferings occurred and which would not have existed had Your sufferings not occurred? But surely those wicked men were not able to do anything except because You freely permitted it; nor did You suffer except because You graciously willed to. And so, I ought to detest the cruelty of those wicked men, to imitate Your sufferings and death by grieving over them, to love Your gracious will by giving thanks, and in these ways to exult, free of distress, over the goods conferred upon me.

Therefore, O insignificant man, leave the cruelty of these men to the judgment of God, and meditate upon what you owe your Savior. Consider what your condition was and what has been done for you; reflect upon how worthy of love is He who has done this for you. Behold your need and His goodness; see what thanks you may give and how much you owe to His love. You were in darkness, on slippery footing, on the downward road to the chaos of Hell, from which there is no return. An enormous lead-like weight hanging from your neck· was causing you to stoop. A burden too heavy for your back was pressing upon you. Invisible foes[20] were urging you onward with all their fury. Such was your helplessness and you did not know it, because you were conceived and born in that condition. O how desperate was that condition! To what a destination these forces were impelling you! Let the memory of it terrify you; tremble at the very thought!

O good Lord Jesus Christ, in this state I was neither seeking nor deliberating; but like the sun You shined forth upon me[21] and showed me my plight. You cast off the leaden weight which was drawing me down; You removed the burden which was pushing me down; You repelled the foes who were impelling me onward, warding them off for my sake. You called me by a new name which You derived from Your name. Stooped over as I was, You stood me upright to face You, saying: "Be confident, I have redeemed You and given my soul [life] for you.[22] If you will cling to me, you will escape the evils of your former condition and will not fall into the abyss toward which you were hastening; instead, I will lead you to my kingdom and will make you an heir of God and a joint-heir with me."[23] Thereafter, You brought me under Your protection so that nothing might harm my soul against its will.[24] And, lo, although I did not yet cling to You as You had exhorted, You did not permit me to fall into Hell. But You awaited the time when I would cling to You and You would do what You had promised.

Yes, O Lord, such was my condition, and these things You have done for me. I was in darkness because I knew nothing – not even my very self. I was on slippery footing because I was weak and prone to sin. I was on the downward road to the chaos of Hell because in our first parents I had descended from justice to injustice (and injustice leads down to Hell), from happiness to the misery of this life (from which one falls into eternal misery). The weight of original sin was dragging me down; the unbearable burden of God's judgment was pushing me down; demons hostile to me were urging me on, as strenuously as they could, so that they might make me deserving of even greater condemnation because of added sins.

Being thus destitute of all help, I was illumined by You and shown my condition. For while I was not yet able to know my condition You taught all these things to others on my behalf, and later You taught these same things to me even before I inquired. You cast aside the leaden weight, the unbearable burden, and the impelling foes, for You removed the sin in which I had been conceived and born,[25] You removed also the condemnation of this sin, and You forbade evil spirits to constrain my soul. You gave me the name Christian, which derives from Your own name; through Your name I confess, and You acknowledge, that I am among the redeemed. You stood me upright and lifted me to the knowledge and love of You. You made me confident of my soul's salvation, for which You gave Your soul [life]. You promised me Your glory if I would follow You. And, behold, while I was not yet following You, as You had exhorted, but was even continuing to commit manifold sins, which You had proscribed, You awaited the time when I would follow You and You would give what You had promised.

Consider, O my soul, peer into, O my inmost being, how much my entire substance owes to Him. Yes, O Lord, because You created me I owe my entire self to Your love; because You redeemed me I owe my entire self; because Your promises are so great I owe my entire self. Indeed, I owe to Your love much more than myself – as much more as You are greater than I, for whom You gave Yourself and to whom You promise Yourself. I pray You, O Lord, make me to taste by loving, what I taste by knowing. Let me sense by affection what I sense by understanding. I owe more than my entire self, but I have no more to give; of myself I am not even able to give my entire self. O Lord, draw my whole self into Your love. The whole of what I am belongs to You as Creator; make it Yours through its loving commitment.

Behold, O Lord, my heart is before You. It strains, but can do nothing of itself;[26] do, O Lord, what it cannot do. Receive me into the inner chamber of Your love. I ask, I seek, I knock.[27] You who cause me to ask, cause me also to receive. You grant that I seek; grant that I also may find. You teach me to knock; open to me when I knock. If You deny to him who asks, to whom do You then give? If he who seeks seeks in vain, who then finds? If You keep [the chamber door] closed for one who knocks, for whom do You open? If You withhold Your love from one who implores, what do You give to one who does not implore? You cause me to desire; cause me also to obtain. O my soul, cling to Him, cling tenaciously. Good Lord, O good Lord, do not scorn my soul, which faints out of hunger for Your love. Revive my soul; let Your tender kindness satisfy it, let Your affection make it fat, let Your love fill it. Let Your love seize my whole being; let it possess me completely, because together with the Father and the Holy Spirit You are the only God, blessed forever.[28] Amen.

ABBREVIATIONS

M   *Monologion*
P   *Proslogion*
DV   *De Veritate*
DL   *De Libertate Arbitrii*
DIV   *Epistola de Incarnatione Verbi*
CDH   *Cur Deus Homo*
DCV   *De Conceptu Virginali et de Originali Peccato*
DP   *De Processione Spiritus Sancti*
DC   *De Concordia Praescientiae et Praedestinationis et Gratiae Dei cum Libero Arbitrio*
PF   *Ein neues unvollendetes Werk des hl. Anselm von Canterbury* (Philosophical Fragments)
DT   *De Trinitate* (Augustine)
PL   *Patrologia Latina* (ed. J. P. Migne)
S   *Sancti Anselmi Opera Omnia* (ed. F. S. Schmitt). E.g., S I, 237:7 indicates Volume I, page 237, line 7.
N   That than which a greater cannot be thought=a necessary being

NOTES

PREFACE

1. For a more detailed analysis of Anselm's intellectual relationship to Augustine, see J. Hopkins, *A Companion to the Study of St Anselm*, Minneapolis: University of Minnesota Press 1972.
2. *Monologion* 15.
3. *Proslogion* 2.
4. Anselm took the statement of this theory from the school of Laon. But he was also directly familiar with Augustine's own statements. See J. Rivière, "D'un singulier emprunt à S. Anselme chez Raoul de Laon," *Revue des sciences religieuses* 16, 1936, 344–6.
5. Attention is called to the short list of corrections printed at the end of these volumes and not found in the earlier Thomas Nelson edition.

MONOLOGION: Preface and Text

1. Cf. DT 1.4.7. In M 79 Anselm's reference to God as three substances may have disturbed some of his readers, since this terminology had become alien to the Latin Church, which insisted that God is one substance. Anselm's concern that the preface be transcribed with the work itself may indicate as well that some readers were puzzled by his dialectic in Chapters 20–24, not understanding the technique of "debating with oneself."
2. Regarding the antecedent of *"illo"* (in *"illo prosequente"* at S I, 13:16) cf. S I, 47:5.
3. Anselm deduces consequences not mentioned in Scripture, which is authoritative. Cf. DC III, 6 (S II, 271:28–272:7).
4. Cf. Augustine's reasoning in DT 8.3.
5. That is, it is good through one thing, not through two things.
6. Throughout M Anselm's argument draws upon this distinction between *esse per se* and *esse per aliud*.
7. This meaning of "greatness" applies to Anselm's description of God (in P 2) as "that than which a greater cannot be thought." Note P 14 (S I, 111:9) and P 18 (S I, 114:21).
8. Anselm is arguing, then, that there cannot be more than one being which, strictly speaking, exists *per se*. In M 44 he distinguishes between existing *per se* and existing *de alio*, and maintains that these are compatible modes of existing. The Son of God exists *through* Himself while existing *from* the Father, because the Son has from the Father the fact of existing through Himself. Yet, in the present chapter Anselm is not drawing upon the *per se/de alio* distinction. According to the present argument

a thing can exist *per se* in some respect without existing *per se* in every respect. As *summa essentia* and *summum esse*, God alone exists absolutely *per se*, for He shares His nature with no other.

9. *"Essentia," "substantia," "natura"* are here (but not everywhere) used interchangeably. N.B. M 26 and 79. See n. 12 below.

10. Cf. Augustine, *City of God* 12.1.3 (PL 41:349).

11. What exists *per se* is the highest being of all. And, conversely, the highest being of all exists *per se*.

12. Anselm uses *"essentia"* sometimes in place of *"esse"* and *"existentia"* and sometimes in place of *"natura"* and *"substantia."* With respect to the former use cf. s I, 189:24 with 188:29 (DV 9); cf. s I, 276:3 with 276:7 (DCD 28); cf. s I, 235:3–4 with 235:7 (DCD I); note also the end of M 6 (s I, 20:15–19) as well as s I, 261:7–8 (DCD 16). With respect to the latter use see M 3 (s I, 16:26–28) and M 4 (s I, 17:17–18 and 17:33); cf. s I, 245:22–24 (DCD 8) with the last half of DCD I. We must remember that *"essentia"* replaces Augustine's word *"natura,"* which sometimes means "natural existent."

In M 4 (s I, 17:14–15) Anselm uses *"essentia"* for *what* a thing is.

Unlike the German word *"Wesen"* the English word "essence" cannot easily serve all of the above purposes. In general, the most accurate English translation of Anselm's *"essentia"* is "being." And at the beginning of DCD 8 Anselm explains that there are many beings (*essentiae*) besides the ones which are properly called substances.

Other relevant references in M are s I, 61:23–24 and s I, 37:10–11. Note PF 42:30; 42:32–33; 43:14–15 – where Anselm interchanges *"non existit in rerum natura," "est absque omni essentia,"* and *"habet nec ullam existentiam."* Note Gaunilo's use of *"essentia"* for "existence" in *On Behalf of the Fool* 6 (s I, 128:30). And, finally, see Augustine's *Catholic and Manichean Ways of Life* 2.2.2 and DT 5.2.3.

13. Anselm takes this division of causes from Cicero's *Topics*. Anselm did not know Boethius's discussion of Cicero's division. See F. S. Schmitt, "Anselm und der (Neu-)Platonismus," *Analecta Anselmiana* I, Frankfurt: Minerva Press 1969, 44.

14. Literally: "Hence, no thing even conceivably preceded – through which thing this Nature existed from nothing."

15. Anselm makes no distinction – either here or elsewhere – between existing and subsisting. In most places *"subsistere"* can be translated as "to exist."

16. *Quemadmodum enim sese habent ad invicem lux et lucere et lucens, sic sunt ad se invicem essentia et esse et ens, hoc est existens sive subsistens. Ergo summa essentia et summe esse et summe ens, id est summe existens sive summe subsistens, non dissimiliter sibi convenient, quam lux et lucere et lucens.*

17. A pun.

18. A pun.

19. Fredegisus († 834) had maintained that the nothingness from which God created the world was other than absolutely nothing (PL 105:752).

20. Note also M 34 (S I, 53:22-24). Anselm takes the doctrine of exemplarism from Augustine. See *Eighty-Three Different Questions* 46.2 (PL 40:30); *On the Gospel of John* 1.17 (PL 35:1387); *Literal Commentary on Genesis* 5.14.31 (PL 34:332).

21. *locutio:* "expression," or "speaking."

22. Concerning the example of the craftsman note P 2 and *On Behalf of the Fool* 3. On the distinction between thinking words and thinking things, see P 4 and *On Behalf of the Fool* 4.

23. Note DT 8.6.9, where Augustine calls mental images *words*. Cf. M 32, n. 71.

24. Cf. CDH II, 11 (S II, 109:8-11): "I think that mortality pertains not to sinless human nature but to corrupt human nature. Indeed, if man had never sinned and if his immortality had been immutably confirmed, he would have been no less a real man; and when mortals will rise in incorruptibility, they will be, no less, real men."

See also CDH I, 9 (S II, 61:25-28); I, 22 (S II, 90:20-23); II, 2 (S II, 98:10-11); II, 3. Note Boethius, *On Aristotle's Categories* (PL 64:163); *On Cicero's Topics* (PL 64:1096). Cf. Augustine, DT 7.4.7; 15.7.11; *On Order* 2.11.31.

25. Cf. DT 14.7.10; 15.10.19.

26. Cf. DT 11.8.14 (PL 42:995).

27. Literally: "which he has drawn into his memory from things known from elsewhere." Cf. Augustine's *Ep.* 7.

28. Rom. 11:36.

29. Note Augustine's distinction between predicating *secundum substantiam, secundum accidens,* and *secundum relationem:* DT 5.3.4 to 5.5.6 (PL 42:912-914). See also DT 5.8.9; 15.5.8; *On the Gospel of John* 22.14; 39.3-4; *Sermon* 244.3.

30. Literally: "Thus, it is evident that its being able to be spoken of relationally as *supreme* over all things or as *greater* than all things which have been created by it (or as something else in like manner) does not designate its natural being."

31. More literally: "just as it is blasphemous to suppose that the substance of the Supreme Nature is something than which the contradictory would in some respect be better, so this substance must be whatever in every respect is better than not that thing."

32. For a discussion of M 15 see Nelson Pike, "The Justification of the Doctrine of Timelessness: Anselm," in his *God and Timelessness*, London: Routledge and Kegan Paul 1970, 130-66.

33. Augustine (DT 5.1.2): "Let us understand God (if we are able, and as best we are able) to be good without quality, great without quantity, Creator without need, ruling from no position, containing all things without Himself being shaped, wholly everywhere without place, everlasting without time, making mutable things without Himself changing, and Himself suffering nothing."

34. DT 6.7.8.

35. Cf. Augustine, *City of God* 11.10.3 (PL 41:326).

36. Ch. 16.

37. Loc. cit.

38. This argument is repeated in DV 1.

39. Anselm is contrasting (1) treating nothing as a kind of being and (2) making a negation of the form "There is no x such that x taught me to fly."

40. Ch. 14.

41. Ch. 18.

42. Anselm begins a dialectical section which concludes with two contradictory statements. Chapters 22–24 attempt to resolve the contradiction.

43. Ch. 16.

44. Ch. 17.

45. Ch. 20.

46. Chs. 18 and 20 respectively.

47. Cf. Augustine, *Confessions* 5.2.

48. See Ch. 14.

49. *Intellectus:* the intellect, the understanding. See P 2, n. 27.

50. See Ch. 18.

51. From Boethius, *Consolation of Philosophy* 5.6 (PL 63:858).

52. Ch. 22.

53. Ch. 17.

54. Cf. DT 5.16.17.

55. Literally: ". . . the Supreme Nature, which neither distributes itself unto many substances nor gathers itself through essential association with any other . . ."

56. This Spirit is a particular, not a universal.

57. Chs. 17 and 25.

58. Note Augustine, *Expositions of the Psalms* 134.4 (PL 37:1741).

59. Literally: ". . . its being is of this kind . . ."

60. Chs. 10–12.

61. Chs. 3, 7, and 13.

62. Literally: "For not like a man does it not always speak what it understands."

63. Ch. 27.

64. See Ch. 27, n. 56.

65. Ch. 12.

66. Note Augustine, *Confessions* 11.7.

67. See Ch. 10, n. 23.

68. Literally: "But perhaps no ambiguity will remain if just as the truth of a man is said to be in the living man, but the likeness or image of that truth [is said to be] in a portrait, so the truth of existing is understood to be in the Word, whose being exists so supremely that, in a way, it alone exists. . . ."

69. Note Augustine, *Eighty-Three Different Questions* 51.2 (PL 40:32–33).

70. On Anselm's view, all thoughts (these he also calls words) that are thoughts of objects are *images* of these objects. They mentally depict these objects. But though the English expression "my thought of x"

makes sense, the expression "my word of x" does not. To preserve the sense of "of" which Anselm has in mind, it seems best to translate "verbum eorum . . ." as "Word [or Image] of those things. . . ." N.B. M 38 (S 1, 56:24–28); M 46 (S 1, 62:22–26); M 63 (S 1, 74: 3–4, 9–10).

71. It is important to notice that Anselm is not discussing words in the usual sense. He is talking about "words by which an object is *thus* mentally spoken" – i.e., about thoughts which "depict" what they are thoughts of. Hence, what he means by "Every word is a word of some thing" is: Every mental image is the image of some thing. And when he declares, "There can be no word of that which neither was, is, nor will be," he is not suggesting the absurd theory that our language can have no words for nonexistent things such as unicorns. Rather, he is stating that an image is not rightly said to be the *image* of some thing unless that thing at some time exists. Cf. M 48 (S 1, 63:20–22); M 63 (S 1, 73:10–12). Note the second sentence of M 31. N.B. Anselm uses "image" and "word" equivocally. E.g., he calls both thoughts and memory-images *words*, as well as calling them both *images* (Cf. M 33, 62, 10).

72. This reasoning is rejected by Anselm.

73. Like Augustine, Anselm uses *"memini"* and *"reminisci"* in a broader sense than the English word "remembering." The Latin verbs encompass *being mindful of, being aware of, being conscious of.* Cf. Eccl. 12:1: "Remember your Creator in the days of your youth."

74. I.e., just as the Word by which the Creator speaks created things is what the Creator is.

75. As the second member of the Trinity, the Word of God is (1) the Image or Likeness of God the Father (Col. 1:15; Heb. 1:3; M 33) and also (2) the eternally begotten Son of God the Father (John 3:16; Heb. 1:5; M 42). Corresponding to these two identifications are two different uses of the genitive in the phrase "Word of God" (*verbum Dei*). This difference can best be seen in English by using two different prepositions. (1) The Word is similar *to* God the Father; (2) the Word is *from* God the Father. In the context above, Anselm is employing "Word of this Spirit" in the first sense: the Word is similar to God the Father (so similar as to be consubstantial with Him) and is the Image of God the Father.

In other passages Anselm switches to the second use of the genitive – even using the phrase *"suum verbum"* [e.g., M 31 (S 1, 48:26); the title of Ch. 34; M 33 (S 1, 53:1–2, 8)].

76. *"Character"* is a Latin transliteration of χαρακτήρ, a word translated in the Vulgate (Heb. 1:3) by *"figura."*

77. Cf. Augustine, *On the Gospel of John* 1.17 (PL 35:1387), and Gaunilo, *On Behalf of the Fool* 3.

78. Cf. Ch. 9.

79. Cf. John 1:3–4.

80. Cf. Col. 1:16.

81. Note Augustine, DT 13.2.5. See also M 43.

82. Ch. 29.

83. "Spirit" is in Latin a masculine noun (*spiritus*); "truth" and "wisdom" are feminine nouns (*veritas, sapientia*).

84. I.e., properties of the Supreme Spirit and its offspring.
85. This same idea is expressed in Ch. 38.
86. Literally: "For not just as a man's wisdom is understood (through which wisdom a man is wise, who cannot be wise through himself) so can there be understood (if the Father is called the essence of the Son and the Son the essence of the Father) that in this way the Son is existent through the Father and the Father through the Son – as if the one could not be existent except through the other, just as a man cannot be wise except through wisdom."
87. Cf. John 5:26.
88. Chs. 27 and 39.
89. Ch. 38.
90. See Ch. 32, n. 73.
91. Anselm subscribes to the *filioque* doctrine. N.B. DP. Augustine also refers to the Father as memory, the Son as understanding, and their Spirit as will, or love (DT 15.7.12).
92. Cf. DP I (S II, 183:22–29).
93. Literally: ". . . no truth allows that . . ."
94. Literally: "No nature permits it to be confirmed by any instance that . . ."
95. "*Spiritus*" means both *spirit* and *breath*. Hence, the one who proceeds from the Father and from the Son can plausibly be called spirit *because* He is breathed out, as it were. Anselm distinguishes the Spirit of the Father and the Son (the Holy Spirit) from the Supreme Spirit (God).
96. I.e., the fact that no one of the three is greater than the other two; that no one of them can exist apart from the others or outside the others.
97. Ch. 59.
98. Literally: "How *there* there is only one of one."
99. Ch. 38.
100. Ch. 29.
101. Chs. 33 and 42.
102. Loc. cit.
103. Cf. CDH I, 25 (S II, 96:2–3).
104. Isa. 53:8.
105. Literally: "But on the other hand, if such is the manner of its ineffability . . ."
106. Ch. 26.
107. Literally: ". . . in words which are common to other natures, the sense is not at all common."
108. Cf. PF (e.g., 34:16 ff.).
109. Anselm subscribes to the doctrine of "analogy of being." Cf. Chs. 31, 66, and 67.
110. I Cor. 13:12.
111–112. Ch. 31.
113. Cf. I Cor. 13:12.
114. I.e., can be conscious of itself. See n. 73 above.
115. Cf. Augustine, *City of God* 22.30.1 (PL 41:801).

116. I Cor. 13:12.

117. Matt. 22:37.

118. The Latin idiom is difficult to capture in English. We have used the following renderings: *tendere in (illam)* – to strive unto; *tendere ad (illam)* – to strive for; *credere in (illam)* – to believe in; *credere ad (illam)* – to believe on.

119. Jas. 2:20, 26.

120. Gal. 5:6.

121. Cf. Boethius, *The Person and the Two Natures* 3 (PL 64:1343).

122. Ch. 26.

123. Ch. 13.

PROSLOGION: Preface and Text

1. M was completed during the second half of 1076. P was probably written about 1077–78. The controversy with Gaunilo occurred in the next year or so. See F. S. Schmitt, "Zur Chronologie der Werke des hl. Anselm von Canterbury," *Revue Bénédictine* 44, 1932, 322–50.

2. Literally: "which would need no other than itself alone for proving itself . . ."

3. Note also Ep. 109.

4. † 1106.

5. Cf. Matt. 6:6; Isa. 26:20.

6. Ps. 26:8 (27:8).

7. I Tim. 6:16.

8. Ps. 50:13 (51:11).

9. Ps. 77:25 (78:25).

10. Ps. 126:2 (127:2).

11. Ps. 121:9 (122:9).

12. Jer. 14:19.

13. Ps. 114:3 (116:3).

14. Ps. 37:9 (38:8).

15. Ps. 6:4; 12:1 (6:3; 13:1).

16. Ps. 12:4 (13:3).

17. Ps. 79:4, 8 (80:3, 7).

18. Ps. 78:9 (79:9).

19. Job 3:24.

20. Ps. 37:5 (38:4).

21. Ps. 68:16 (69:15).

22. See M 67 (S I, 78:9); M 32 n. 73.

23. Cf. Isa. 7:9. Anselm takes this reading from Augustine, who follows an Old Latin translation of the Septuagint. See DT 5.2.2. As *Christian Doctrine* 2.12.17 attests, Augustine was not unaware of the alternative translation: "Unless you believe, you will not continue" (*Si non credideritis, non permanebitis*).

24. Cf. Heb. 11:6.

25. Ps. 13:1; 52:1 (14:1; 53:1).

26. By "greater" Anselm means "better," "more perfect," "more excellent." Note M 2 (S I, 15:19–20); P 14 (S I, 111:9); P 18 (S I, 114:21).

Notes

27. Obviously *"in* the understanding" is not to be construed spatially. This phrase is idiomatic for Anselm in the way that "to have something *in* mind" is idiomatic for us. Anselm uses *"intellectus"* to indicate, variously, (1) an act of understanding, (2) intelligence (*Reply to Gaunilo* 2. s 1, 132:12–13), (3) a capability, or power, of the soul (*Reply to Gaunilo* 2. s 1, 132:19–20. Also M 23. s 1, 41:28–29), (4) a meaning or respect (*Reply to Gaunilo* 2. s 1, 132: 29–30. Also M 19. s 1, 34:19–21).

What is understood (for an act of understanding) is understood by the understanding (a capability of the soul) and is therefore in the understanding (a manner of speaking). Because reflective thinking is an operation of the rational soul, understanding (which is a mode of thinking) is also an operation of the soul.

28. Cf. M 10 and *On Behalf of the Fool* 3.

29. Anselm is developing a single line of reasoning (*unum argumentum*). That is, he 'establishes' the existence and nature of God by spelling out what is involved in the single notion *that than which a greater cannot be thought.* P 2 presents the existence proof, which takes the form of a *reductio ad impossibile.* Using the same form, P 3 then argues for God's uniqueness, while P 4 explains in what sense it is possible for someone to deny that God exists – given (from P 3) that he cannot conceive of God as not existing. The remaining chapters 'demonstrate' and discuss the major attributes of God.

P 2 has come to be called Anselm's ontological argument. This label is not Anselm's but derives from the period of Kant (though it is not original with Kant). In the *Critique of Pure Reason* Kant attacks the "ontological" arguments of Gottfried Wilhelm von Leibniz and Christian Wolff, whose formulations are different from Anselm's. Also, Anselm does not speak of God as *ens realissimum* but refers to Him as *summa essentia* (M 16), *summum esse* (M 19), *aliquid quo nihil maius cogitari potest* (P 2).

30. Anselm, like Augustine, subscribes to a theory of degrees of reality (note M 28, 31, and 34). God is more real, exists more, than do created things.

31. Ps. 13:1; 52:1 (14:1; 53:1).

32. Literally: "either without any signification or with some strange signification."

33. Literally: "that God exists in this manner . . ."

34. This paragraph is the conclusion for Chs. 2–4 and not merely for Ch. 4.

In CHD I, 1 (S II, 48: 19–24) Boso indicates that he would continue to believe even if he could not understand. Anselm does not call upon Boso to suspend his belief but to suspend appeal to his belief in order to prove by rational necessity (*rationes necessariae*) that the Son of God became incarnate. Anselm's "rationalism" is therefore a methodological rationalism, as Schmitt indicates ("Die wissenschaftliche Methode in Anselms 'Cur Deus homo'," *Spicilegium Beccense*, Paris 1959, 349–70). The same methodology obtains in M and P.

35. See M 15 and *Reply to Gaunilo* 10 for a statement of this same principle.

36. Peter Damian (1007–1072) had raised the question about whether

God could make what has happened not to have happened. See *De Divina Omnipotentia* (PL 145:618–620).

37. Note PF 24:16; DV 8; DCD 12; CDH II:17.

38. Note PF 26:23ff.

39. Note PF 43:20–23.

40. *"Iustus"* and *"iustitia"* mean *just* and *justice* in the sense of *righteous* and *righteousness*.

41. I Tim. 6:16.

42. Ps. 24:10; 144:17 (25:10; 145:17).

43. See M 15 and *Reply to Gaunilo* 10.

44. Cf. M 16.

45. Ps. 42:3 (43:3).

46. Cf. I John 3:2.

47. Cf. I John 1:5.

48. See M 65.

49. I Tim. 6:16.

50. Acts 17:28.

51. *Turbatio* Jer. 14:19.

52. Cf. Ps. 50:10 (51:8).

53. Ps. 50:7 (51:5).

54. Rom. 5:12.

55. Cf. Ps. 24:7 (25:7).

56. Ps. 26:9 (27:9).

57. Ps. 12:4 (13:3).

58. Cf. S. of Sol. 6:13.

59. Cf. M 22.

60. Ps. 89:2 (90:2). Cf. M 19.

61. Cf. M 15.

62. Literally: "Is this, then, the age of the age or the ages of ages?" Scripture uses the phrases *"in saeculum saeculi"* (singular) and *"in saecula saeculorum"* (plural) to express eternity, or what is forever and ever, "world without end." Cf. Ps. 111:9 (112:9) with I Pet. 4:11, e.g. In P 21 Anselm questions whether or not there are numerically different eternities in God. The issue is explored more fully in DIV 15 and DP 16.

63. Note M 14 and 23.

64. See Ch. 3, n. 30.

65. Ex. 3:14.

66. Cf. M 42, where the Word is identified as the Son.

67. Cf. M 49–50.

68. Luke 10:42. Note Augustine, *Sermon* 103.3.4 (PL 38:614–15), *Sermon* 255.6.6 (PL 38:1189).

69. Cf. P 18, where God is called every true good. Note also P 22. Cf. Augustine, *City of God* 22.30.1 (PL 41:801).

70. Cf. Augustine, *Catholic and Manichean Ways of Life* 1.3.4 (PL 32:1312): "In my opinion, a man cannot be called happy (1) if he does not have what he loves, regardless of what it is, or (2) if he has what he loves but it is harmful to him, or (3) if he does not love what he has, though it be good for him."

71. I Cor. 2:9.
72. Matt. 13:43.
73. Matt. 22:30.
74. I Cor. 15:44.
75. Wisd. 5:15.
76. Ps. 36:39 (37:39).
77. Ps. 16:15 (17:15).
78. Ps. 35:9 (36:8).
79. Loc. cit.
80. Cf. John 14:21.
81. Cf. Matt. 22:37-39.
82. Cf. Matt. 25:21, 23.
83. Matt. 5:9.
84. Cf. John 10:32.
85. John 14:3.
86. Rom. 8:17.
87. Rom. 8:38-39.
88. Matt. 22:37.
89. John 16:24.
90. Matt. 25:21.
91. I Cor. 2:9.
92. John 16:24.
93. Isa. 9:6.
94. Cf. Ps. 62:2 (63:1).
95. Matt. 25:21.
96. Rom. 1:25.

ON BEHALF OF THE FOOL

1. Early mss. do not contain Gaunilo's name. See s 1, 125 n.
2. Ps. 13:1; 52:1 (14:1; 53:1).
3. Most of the early mss. do not contain these divisions. See s 1, 125 n.
4. Gaunilo here misstates Anselm's argument. Anselm does not argue that if N (=that than which a greater cannot be thought=a necessary being) does not exist, then *any* existing being is greater than N. He argues that if N did not exist, N could be thought to exist, and thus could be thought to be greater than it is – a contradiction. In the example of the perfect island (Section 6) Gaunilo states the point differently: "If [this island] did not exist, then any other really existing country would be more excellent than it, and thus this island, which has already been understood by you to be more excellent [than all other lands] would not be more excellent [than all others]." That is, Gaunilo does *not* here argue: "If this island did not exist, anything at all which does exist would be greater than it."
5. Gaunilo switches from the description "a nature than which nothing greater can be thought" to the description "that which is greater than all others" (*maius omnibus*). Probably he intended *"maius omnibus"* as an abbreviation of *"illud maius omnibus quae cogitari possunt"*: "that which

is greater than all others that can be thought" (See the beginning and end of Section 4. S I, 126:30 and 127:23. Also note S I, 126:26–27). But Anselm reads *"maius omnibus"* as a shorthand for *"maius omnibus quae sunt"*: "that which is greater than all other existing beings" (S I, 135:8–10); he therefore remonstrates with Gaunilo over confusing the expression *"N"* with the expression *"maius omnibus."* And, indeed, Gaunilo does once use the description *"maior natura omnium quae sunt"* (Section 7. S I, 129:8). But here he is not employing it as a substitute for Anselm's formula (as he *does* use *"maius omnibus quae cogitari possunt"* substitutionally). Rather, he is calling upon Anselm to abandon his *Proslogion* 2 argument, regarded as fallacious, in favor of a sound argument to show that there really exists a being greater than all others, viz., God.

Both Gaunilo and Anselm understand the word *"aliis"* as supplied in the phrase *"maius omnibus [aliis]."* Gaunilo also omits *"aliis"* when talking about an island greater than all *others*, though he obviously intends for the reader to supply this word (S I, 128:22). Anselm himself, like all medieval writers, did not always explicitly add *"aliud"* to contexts where it obviously belonged. E.g., M 64 (S I, 75:7).

6. Sections 2–4 deal mainly with the question of how that than which a greater cannot be thought is in the understanding. Sections 5–6 attack the claim that this nature exists also in reality. The first half of Section 7 responds to P 3; and the second half speaks for Gaunilo himself (not for the Fool) in recommending that P 3 describe God as "not able to be *understood* not to exist."

The general outline of Gaunilo's attack is, then:

A. Section 1: recapitulation of Anselm's argument.
B. Sections 2–4.

    1. Gaunilo requires Anselm to prove that N does not exist in the way that unreal objects do [2].

    2. Anselm's comparison with the craftsman, or artist, is wrong [3].

    3. The words "that which is greater than all others that can be thought" are thinkable, but what they signify is not thinkable [4].

C. Sections 5–7½.

    1. Anselm's argument begs the question by maintaining: if this being (described as greater than all others) did not exist, it would not be greater than all others; therefore, it exists (Gaunilo does not comprehend the *reductio* structure of the argument) [5].

    2. Anselm's procedure is as absurd as contending that a perfect island exists because it can be conceived or understood [6].

    3. N can be thought not to exist [7].

D. Sections 7½–8.

    1. Anselm should say that N cannot be *understood* not to exist, for surely N can be *thought* not to exist [7].

    2. Concluding remarks [8].

7. Gaunilo is not here proposing to substitute "understand" for "think" in Anselm's argument. Rather, he is surmising that Anselm might intend this move. Gaunilo's dialectic may be summarized as follows:

Notes

A. Speaking on behalf of the unbelieving Fool:

1. If the criterion for having something in the understanding is that someone's words are understood, then all manner of falsehoods and unreal things are in the understanding. So N might be understanding and still not exist in reality.

2. Moreover, if you, Anselm, were to say that N is in the understanding in such way that N must be understood to exist, then the distinction between understanding and understanding to exist collapses, in the case of N, making your example of the artist irrelevant.

3. Indeed, I deny that, properly speaking, N is in my understanding (i.e., is understood), because I have no acquaintance either with N itself or with anything of the same species or genus.

B. Speaking for myself, the believing monk (Section 7):

I reject your criterion for something's being in the understanding. It is not the case that x is in my understanding simply because I understand what someone says about x. Rather, x is in my understanding and is understood only if in conjunction with my thinking x, x is really the case, so that my thought of x is true. Since I am sure that God exists, I deem it more appropriate (as should you) to say that God is understood to exist and cannot be understood not to exist (than to say that He cannot be *thought* not to exist).

Just as *Reply to Gaunilo* 4 speaks to *On Behalf of the Fool* 7, so Anselm's Section 6 takes issue with Gaunilo's Section 2. But Anselm misunderstands Gaunilo's dialectic and therefore charges Section 2 with a blatant inconsistency.

8. *On the Gospel of John* 1.17 (PL 35:1387). See M 9 and 34.

9. Gaunilo is distinguishing between imagining something (viz., a painting) which does not yet exist and conceiving of something (viz., N) which is alleged already to exist.

10. In fact, however, Anselm subscribes to the doctrine of "analogy of being." See M 31, M 65–67.

11. See M 10 and P 4.

12. That is, Gaunilo thinks that Anselm's argument begs the question of God's existence. Yet, even if Anselm does beg the question, Gaunilo does not really discern the *reductio ad impossibile* structure of the argument.

13. Literally: "of finding what does not exist."

14. See n. 4.

15. Having finished with the Fool's response, Gaunilo now speaks for himself. Thus, he can say: "I understand indubitably that that being which is supreme, viz., God, exists and cannot fail to exist."

16. That is, the Fool thinks a proposition which both Anselm and Gaunilo regard as a falsehood, viz., that God does not exist. But, maintains Gaunilo, the Fool cannot *understand* this falsehood because, strictly speaking, only truths can be understood.

157

Notes

REPLY TO GAUNILO

1. Most early mss. do not contain the subsequent divisions into sections (See s 1, 130n.). At the beginning of Section 5 Anselm indicates that his reply deals first with Gaunilo's more important objections and later with those so obviously wrong as not really to need refuting. Thus, Anselm's response does not follow the order of Gaunilo's criticisms.

The outline of the *Reply* is, then:

A. Sections 1–4.
    1. If N can be thought to exist, N exists [1].
    2. If N can even be thought, N exists [1].
    3. N exists everywhere and always [1].
    4. Restatement of the argument of P 2, emphasizing the *reductio* structure of the proof [2].
    5. "Reply" to the perfect-island objection [3].
    6. Restatement of the argument of P 3: N cannot be thought not to exist [3].
    7. Rejection of Gaunilo's recommendation to replace "the Supreme Being cannot be *thought* not to exist" by "the Supreme Being cannot be *understood* not to exist" [4].
B. Sections 5–10.
    1. N is a concept having more deductive power than does the concept *that which is greater than all others* [5].
    2. Anselm charges Gaunilo with inconsistency [6].
    3. Anselm discusses the disparity between his claim that N cannot be thought not to exist and the Fool's conviction that God can be thought not to exist [7].
    4. Anselm states his purpose in having introduced the analogy of the artist [8].
    5. Anselm explains how the Fool can acquire a concept of N [8] and states that the Fool's denial of N's existence presupposes that the Fool understands the concept *N* (Otherwise the Fool does not understand what he is denying.) [9].
    6. Statement about God's nature [10].
    7. Concluding remarks [10].

2. Anselm does not seem to know the name or identity of the defender of the Fool. Nor does Eadmer (*Vita Anselmi*) mention Gaunilo by name or location. See *On Behalf of the Fool*, n. 1.

3. That is, Anselm replies to the Christian rather than to the Fool by taking for granted that God is correctly described as that than which a greater cannot be thought and that Gaunilo understands this description. Still, in Section 8 Anselm does reply also to the Fool by explaining how N can in some respects be conceived by reference to created things.

4. Literally: "Let us assume that it does not exist if it can be even thought." But what Anselm means is made clear by the very next sentence ("Now, whatever . . ."), of which the first sentence is a substitution instance.

5. Cf. n. 4.

Notes

6. I.e., if it could be thought not to exist . . .
7. That is,
  (1) For any object x, if there is some time or place at which x does not exist as a whole, then x can be thought not to exist – even if x does exist. (premise)

Thus, (2) if there is some time or place at which N does not exist as a whole, then N can be thought not to exist – even if N does exist. (instance of (1))

But (3) it is not the case that N can be thought not to exist – even if N does exist.
  (a) What cannot be thought not to exist is greater than what can be thought not to exist. (presupposition)
So, (b) if N can be thought not to exist, N can be thought to be greater than it is.
But (c) it is not the case that N can be thought to be greater than it is.
So, (d) it is not the case that N can be thought not to exist.

Hence, (4) it is not the case that there is some time or place at which N does not exist as a whole.

8. Cf. M 65.
9. *In nullo intellectu* (S 1, 132:14–15). Comparison of S 1, 136:28–30 with S 1, 137:2–3 makes clear the nuances of this phrase.

N.B. the phrases *"nec actu nec intellectu potest non esse," "potest vel actu vel intellectu non esse," "vel actu vel intellectu dissolvi potest,"* and *"nec cogitatione potest non esse."* (See S 1, 131:8; 131:10; 114:20–21; 104:3–4 respectively.) In the English translation of these expressions no difference between *intellectu* and *cogitatione* is called for. Both words are accurately translated as "conceivably." Note also M 6 (S 1, 19:23; 20:1, 3–4).

10. Loc. cit.
11. *In ullo intellectu.* See n. 9.
12. Literally: "of finding what does not exist."
13. The reason is that for N to be thought not to exist involves, claims Anselm, an inconsistency.
14. We can *imagine* (a mode of thinking) that something does not exist though *knowing* (another mode of thinking) that it does; but we cannot in the same respect think that it does not exist while thinking that it does exist.
15. P 4.
16. Literally: "The former [inference] needs a premise other than the fact that [this being] is called greater than all others; but in the latter case there is need for no other premise than the fact that [this being] is called that than which a greater cannot be thought."
17. Literally: "Therefore, if what 'that than which a greater cannot be thought' proves about itself by means of itself cannot in the same way be proved about what is called greater than all others, you unjustly criticize me for having said something I did not say. . . ."
18. That is, Anselm is professing that there is a unique case where it *is* possible to derive an existence-statement from a description.
19. Cf. *On Behalf of the Fool* 2 (S 1, 125:20–126:1). Anselm repeats

Gaunilo's phrase "*non [posse] hoc aliter cogitare, nisi intelligendo id est scientia comprehendendo re ipsa illud existere.*" But Anselm's continuation shows that he is understanding this phrase differently from Gaunilo (and thus we have translated it differently in the two cases). For Anselm interprets Gaunilo to be defining "*intelligere*" as "*scientia comprehendere re ipsa illud existere.*" But what Gaunilo did was to construe "*intelligere*" as "*scientia comprehendere*"; he thus identified *intelligere re ipsa illud existere* with *scientia comprehendere re ipsa illud existere*. Gaunilo's meaning would stand out better with the use of parentheses: *non [posse] hoc aliter cogitare, nisi intelligendo (id est scientia comprehendendo) re ipsa illud existere.*

For the structure of Gaunilo's argument see *On Behalf of the Fool*, n. 7.

20. Cf. Matt. 27:4.

21–22. See n. 9.

23. Literally: ". . . so that I could show that something which is not understood to exist is in the understanding."

24. Rom. 1:20.

25. See P 5 and M 15 for a statement of this same principle. Anselm's single line of reasoning (*unum argumentum*) aims at deriving, from the concept of N, the statement of God's existence and various statements about His nature.

A MEDITATION ON HUMAN REDEMPTION

1. Like Augustine (e.g., PL 34:517, 521, 588), Anselm uses "*anima*" to signify *homo*. Both men teach that the soul never dies. They also use "*anima*" to signify *vita*, since the soul is the principle of life.

This meditation was written between 1099–1100. See Eadmer, *The Life of St Anselm*, ed. and trans. by R. W. Southern, London: Thomas Nelson and Sons 1962, p. 122.

2. Ps. 139:8 (140:7).

3. Ps. 18:11; 118:103 (19:10; 119:103).

4. Hab. 3:4 (Vulgate). In the Old Testament horns symbolize strength.

5. Cf. II Cor. 12:9.

6. John 12:32.

7. CDH I, 7.

8. "*Iustitia*" means *justice* in the sense of *righteousness*.

9. CDH I, 8.

10. Cf. CDH I, 5.

11. CDH I, 21.

12. That is, something greater than everything other than God.

13. CDH II, 6.

14. CDH II, 14. N.B. Anselm teaches that the putting of Jesus to death is forgivable because it was done in ignorance that He was messiah (CDH II, 15).

15. Anselm here speaks as if he regarded human nature as an unindividuated universal. Yet, he makes clear elsewhere that he views each man as having a numerically distinct nature. See DIV 11 (S II, 29:4–12 and 29:26–30:6).

16. John 10:18; 15:10.
17. Phil. 2:8.
18. John 14:31. Cf. CDH I, 9–10.
19. John 18:11.
20. Cf. Eph. 6:12.
21. Cf. Ps. 79:4, 8 (80:3, 7).
22. Cf. Matt. 9:22.
23. Rom. 8:17.
24. Cf. P 25 (S I, 119:18–19).
25. Ps. 50:7 (51:5).
26. Cf. John 15:5.
27. Matt. 7:7.
28. *In saecula saeculorum.* Cf. P 21, n. 62.